The Tao of Willie

# of Willie

A GUIDE
TO THE HAPPINESS
IN YOUR
HEART

By
Willie Nelson
with Turk Pipkin

GOTHAM BOOKS

GOTHAM BOOKS
Published by Penguin Group (USA) Inc.
375 Hudson Street, New York, New York 10014, U.S.A.

Penguin Group (Canada), 90 Eglinton Avenue East, Suite 700, Toronto, Ontario M4P 2Y3, Canada
(a division of Pearson Penguin Canada Inc.); Penguin Books Ltd, 80 Strand, London WC2R 0RL,
England; Penguin Ireland, 25 St Stephen's Green, Dublin 2, Ireland (a division of Penguin Books Ltd);
Penguin Group (Australia), 250 Camberwell Road, Camberwell, Victoria 3124, Australia (a division of
Pearson Australia Group Pty Ltd); Penguin Books India Pvt Ltd, 11 Community Centre, Panchsheel
Park, New Delhi – 110 017, India; Penguin Group (NZ), cnr Airborne and Rosedale Roads, Albany,
Auckland 1310, New Zealand (a division of Pearson New Zealand Ltd); Penguin Books (South
Africa) (Pty) Ltd, 24 Sturdee Avenue, Rosebank, Johannesburg 2196, South Africa

Penguin Books Ltd, Registered Offices: 80 Strand, London WC2R 0RL, England

Published by Gotham Books, a division of Penguin Group (USA) Inc.

First printing, May 2006
10   9   8   7   6   5   4   3   2   1

Permissions appear on page 187 and constitute an extension of the copyright page.

Gotham Books and the skyscraper logo are trademarks of Penguin Group (USA) Inc.

LIBRARY OF CONGRESS CATALOGING-IN-PUBLICATION DATA
Nelson, Willie, 1933–
The Tao of Willie : a guide to the happiness in your heart / by Willie Nelson & Turk Pipkin.
    p.   cm.
ISBN 1-592-40197-X (hardcover : alk. paper)
1. Conduct of life.   2. Nelson, Willie, 1933–   I. Pipkin, Turk.   II. Title.
BJ1581.2.N43   2006
170'.44—dc22   2005023091

Printed in the United States of America
Set in Apollo
Designed by Alice Sorensen

Contents 🖋

The Tao
⌖ of Willie

When something positive occurs,
it contains within it
the seeds of negative and positive.
　　—The Tao Te Ching

Once you replace negative thoughts
with positive ones,
you'll start having positive results.
　　—Willie Nelson

The Time of the Teacher 🖋

An Introduction by Turk Pipkin

Some things never change.

Just like when we were kids playing games on a warm summer evening, the world is still comprised of two basic types of people—hiders and seekers. Hiders are generally happy right where they are, while seekers are more likely to look for something new. In our hearts, most of us know which one we are.

There is also a third type of person—the master, one who teaches, inspires, and shows the way for the rest of us. In a game of hide-and-seek, a master will never be found (at least until they want to be).

Those of us on the student side of life—hiders and seekers alike—need teachers to smooth life's bumpy path, or to help us laugh at ourselves when we veer off course and land on our asses. If you're thinking that doesn't apply to you because you haven't landed on your ass lately, just wait. You will.

My name is Turk Pipkin, and I'd known Willie Nelson twenty years before I realized how much I'd learned from him—two decades before I realized that without his even trying, he'd been showing me the way all along. For me, Willie has been that rarest of people—a teacher.

There was a time, of course, when Willie was a student like the rest of us. But I think that somewhere along the way, he found himself on a higher path, so to speak. *The Tao of Willie* is a stroll along that path with a Texas boy who was born with an old soul, and whose heart seems to grow younger with each passing year.

Now before you go thinking I'm gay for the guy, let's get one thing straight. I'm not setting Willie up to be some kind of prophet, to have infallible judgment, or to be sneaking up on perfection. After all, I've seen his golf swing.

I've also seen firsthand as Willie weathered his own share of bumps and falls. And one of the greatest lessons I've learned from him is the value of picking yourself up, dusting off your butt, and getting back on the road again.

Perhaps the best I can say of Willie Hugh Nelson is that no one I know has laughed harder or loved life more.

And if you really want to learn something, what could be better than how to laugh and love?

According to the ancient Chinese philosophy of the *Tao Te Ching*, it is possible to look into one man's eyes and see the entire universe. As a longtime friend and Willie's coauthor of this little book of thoughts and wisdom, I've had the opportunity to look into Willie's eyes—and into the thoughts that give those eyes their shine.

Many of Willie's thoughts are more Baptist than Buddhist, some more cowboy than Indian, but all have stood the test of time through Willie's achievements as a family man, as a friend to everyone he meets, as a believer in justice and freedom, and as one of the great legends of American music.

It would—and will—take an entire book of wit and wisdom to give a fair account of what Willie the student has learned, but first I offer my own brief accounting of a few things I've learned from him.

Call it my "Ode to Willie" (who knows, maybe I am gay for the guy).

Willie Nelson is an American icon. His voice as comforting as the American landscape, his songs as familiar as the color of the sky, his face as worn as the Rocky Mountains. Perhaps that's why it's been suggested we add his face to the cliffs of Mount Rushmore and be done with it.

For half a century, he's played countless concerts across America and around the world. His appeal crosses nearly all social and economic lines, and he's been instrumental in shaping both country and pop music. He's called an outlaw, though from Farm Aid to the aftermath of September 11, from the resurrection of a burned-out courthouse in his own hometown to fanning the flame of the Olympics, it is Willie Nelson who brings us together.

"If America could sing with one voice," said Emmylou Harris, "it would be Willie's."

Willie Nelson is a Highwayman. He may have traded his horse for a tour bus, but he still rides into your town, kidnaps your girl's heart, and pockets just enough of your cash to keep his life in order. And you can hardly wait for him to come back and do it all again next year.

It helps if people love you. Another lesson from the master.

Willie Nelson is a joker. After years on the road, he knows thousands of jokes, and can at any given time remember three. All three, by the way, will make you laugh. Come back next Wednesday and you'll get three more.

Here's the last one he tossed out at me.

"A skeleton walks into a bar and says, 'Give me a beer and a mop.' "

If you don't get it, read it again. It must be funny; I'm still telling it.

Laugh, and don't give a damn whether the world laughs with you.

Willie Nelson has music in his heart. On the radio or in concert, Willie can reach out and touch you. He can set a life back on track with the sound of his voice or the proceeds of his fame, can soothe the madness in your brain with a plaintive Gypsy chord progression, or spark love like a wildfire from a single burning ember. He's cut 250 albums, written 2,500 songs, and sold 50 million records.

As we say in Texas, "That ain't mice nuts."

Willie Nelson has changed the lives of thousands of people, including my own. More important, Willie Nelson also changed HIS life—and I do mean for the better. After beating his hard head against the music business in Nashville during the fifties and sixties, Willie was on hard times. He'd long ago sold some of his best songs—like "Night Life" and "Family Bible"—for a few tens in folding money. His house in Nashville had burned down, and he was sick and tired of trying to be something that he was not.

Making the wisest decision of his life, Willie decided that he cared more about his family, friends, and simply making music than he did about trying to be a star. Moving home to Texas, he wrapped himself in a cocoon of indifference to other people's opinions, and eventually unfolded his new wings and soared.

Willie puts it a little more simply.

"When I started counting my blessings," he says, "my whole life turned around."

Before long, Willie had helped to heal one of America's greatest divides by inspiring hippies and rednecks to realize they weren't all that different from each other. The next thing we knew, the rednecks had grown their hair out, the hippies were wearing boots, and you couldn't tell them apart anymore. He may yet do the same thing for Democrats and Republicans, though I don't advise that you hold your breath on this one.

Like the Chinese masters of the Tao Te Ching, *Willie learned that when you put your life in a good place, good things follow.*

If you spend enough time around Willie and watch how easy he is in the company of everyone from billionaires to bums, you sometimes suspect that he's some kind of chameleon. But the truth is, Willie's the same person no matter who he's with. He can talk to a congressional leader about farm policy, and an hour later he'll be jamming with a punk rock band.

By being true to what is unique about himself, he connects each of us to the best parts of ourselves.

No less amazing is his ability to shine in many different situations. Having played as many as fifty-four holes of golf with him on a single day, I've long wondered how a guy whose swing looks like he's fly casting a frozen turkey can so often walk away the winner.

"If you care too much," Willie once told me on the golf course, "you'll screw up every time."

Whether he was talking about golf or life, I'm not exactly sure.

Willie Nelson is a gambler. Willie has learned how to sit opposite you at a chessboard with a smile on his face and cut you to ribbons, using surprise openings, sneak attacks, and subtle psychology to goad you into a sense of overconfidence that will be over all too soon. The hallmark of a game of chess with Willie is that—whether in the opening, middle, or endgame—you'll think you're doing just fine right up to the point that you realize you're screwed.

Watch out for the Red-Headed Stranger.

Sum it up and you've got a wise guy musical poet who is both yin and yang, heads and tails, Indian and cowboy, a hero to city slickers and to country bumpkins, a prophet, a preacher, a poet, and despite the lyrics to Kris Kristofferson's song, NOT a problem when he's stoned.

The subtle yet simple lessons of the *Tao Te Ching* are a nice match for the simple philosophy that seems to keep Willie on course in his life, a philosophy that can help all of us find happiness through simply being.

"We're going to keep doing it wrong," says Willie, *"until we like it that way."*

Is he joking? Sure. But in that joke, Willie demonstrates a good grasp of the Tao. He's going to do things his way, even if you think his way is a little weird.

Who knows, you may be a Taoist yourself and not even know it. If you put on your boots before you put on your pants because you like it that way, then you're at one with the Tao (or you have small feet and a great big butt).

There is no single definition of the Tao, but I like to think of it as finding a balance between resistance and surrender.

If you try to walk against the current in a flowing stream, for instance, your journey will be a constant struggle. If you lose your footing and are carried away by the current, no matter how you struggle, you may drown.

But if you float with the current, you will become a part of the river and will be carried on an incredible ride. In the same way, if you let yourself join the river of life, you will be carried on an amazing journey.

The river starts here. And Willie Nelson is our guide. Shall we wade into the water?

Turk Pipkin, 2005

He's a carved-in-granite, samurai poet warrior Gypsy guitar-pickin' wild man with a heart as big as Texas and the greatest sense of humor in the West.

—Kris Kristofferson,
   speaking about his friend Willie

Hello. I'm Willie Nelson 🎵

A Way can be a guide, but not a fixed path.
    —The *Tao Te Ching*

Hi. I'm Willie Nelson, and it's a pleasure to meet you. I've met many of you before, of course, out on the road as I've traveled across America and around the world playing my music.

I've seen you at concerts and in honky-tonks. I've seen you in little country churches, at gigantic music festivals, and at countless fund-raisers for causes that we believe in. We may have traded smiles in a café. I might have laughed at a joke you told me, or I may have told you one of mine. Here's one now:

What did the Minnesotan say to the Pillsbury Doughboy?
"Nice tan."

If we both get a laugh out of a quick one like that, then we're ahead of the game. You may even find some deeper meaning in that joke—some analogy to the greater lessons or mysteries of life. (If you do, let me know immediately. As far as I know, it's just a joke . . . but I could be wrong.)

Whether we've been eye to eye, or you've just heard me singing my songs, I'd like to think that we're old friends, new friends, or just friends in the making.

The Texas golf master Harvey Penick said, *"If you play golf, you are my friend."* So what I say is, *"If you love music, you are my friend." It's good to have a lot of friends.*

This book is my way of sharing a little of what I've learned in seventy-two years of making music and friends on this beautiful planet. I don't know if the things I write here will change your life, but they sure changed mine.

The ways my life has changed seem pretty amazing to me, for somewhere along the way, the freckle-faced, dirt-eating kid from Abbott, Texas, ended up being a father, grandfather, and great-grandfather with a family, friends, and work I wouldn't trade for anything on earth. By hook or by crook, I seem to have stumbled onto something all of us search for in this great mystery of life.

Some would call it happiness, but I like to think that what I found is me. That sounds simple enough, but the truth is, it took quite a while to do it. Among other things, it took me learning that I had to quit trying to be someone else.

Trying to be someone else is the hardest road there is.

I thought I'd tell you a little about how I got here, and maybe by getting to know me and a little about the path I've taken, you'll find a path of your own. Along the way, you'll get to know both of us a little better.

That's what we're talking about—me and you.

So welcome to *The Tao of Willie*, my little guide to the happiness in your own heart. From the get-go, we need to get one thing straight. If you're looking for a scholarly work about the ancient Eastern philosophy found in the *Tao Te Ching*, this may not be what you had in mind.

On the other hand, if you don't know beans about the ancient Chinese philosophy called the Tao, there's no reason to fret.

You don't have to know the Tao for the Tao to know you.

Whatever you think of the Tao, if my thoughts strike that bell of truth in your heart, it will also be ringing in mine.

That's the way it is between friends.

What Is It? ↝

What is gooder than God?
More evil than the devil?
The rich need it
The poor have it
And if you eat it you will die?
    —a riddle

Before I give you the answer to that "gooder than God" riddle, we need to consider one important question: *What the *#*@! is a Tao?*

I thought you'd never ask.

The Tao—pronounced "tao" or "dao" depending on how hip you want to sound—is a philosophy of life based on a Chinese text called the *Tao Te Ching*, or "The Way and Its Power."

The *Tao Te Ching* is the work of several writers who were inspired by the teachings of a guy named Lao Tzu, who lived about six hundred years before Christ. But the ideas behind the Tao are older still, and were very likely derived from some of man's oldest teachings.

Like all of life, the Tao is an eternal mystery, and has so much meaning that it may be easier to say what it is not.

The Tao is NOT a religion.
It has no gods, and could be as helpful to a Christian or a Jew

as to a druid who worships trees, a narcissist who worships himself, or a record executive who worships money. Truthfully, the record exec is probably the person who most needs the Tao.

Once you know what the Tao is *not*, then everything else *is* the Tao.

The Tao is the biggest thing there is.

The Tao connects the personal with the universal. It is the link between you and other people. It is the link between you and the natural world, the link between you and the universe. The Tao is the link between you and yourself.

And that ain't all. The Tao is a way of life, a science and an art. It is the natural order, and it is a path that leads to peace and freedom. The Tao is the deepest well of the purest water, but you cannot see it or hear it, touch it or taste it. You also cannot use it up.

The general idea is that if you live your life in accordance with your own essential nature, then your life will be empowered by the Tao.

When Shakespeare wrote, "To thine own self be true," he was dipping into the Tao . . . or into some really good snuff.

The opposite of the Tao would be to live your life in defiance of your original nature, in which case your chances of finding tranquility are pretty much shot to shit.

If you live *according* to the Tao, you live in accordance with the natural world, with other people, and yourself.

If you live in *opposition* to the Tao, your life will unfold in opposition to the natural world, to other people, and to yourself.

The choice is up to you.

If you read this guide distilled from my view of life, love, and laughter, then find yourself wanting more, you will have missed the essence of the Tao, which relies not in wanting more, but in needing less.

"To know you have enough," says the Tao, *"is to be truly rich."*

Like any good philosophy, the Tao is a search for knowledge.
Where do you get this knowledge? When I was a kid, sometimes a feller would be reluctant to say where he'd gotten something—like, say, a "borrowed" horse—so he'd say he got it "from the getting place."

But before we get to the getting place, what about my riddle? What is gooder than God and more evil than the devil, that the rich need and the poor have, and if you eat it you will die?

The answer, of course, is "nothing."

Lessons Learned in Abbott 🖎

I can see us sitting 'round the table
When from the family Bible Dad would read.
And I can hear my mother softly singing
Rock of Ages, Rock of Ages, cleft for me.
    —Willie Nelson, "Family Bible"

In Abbott, Texas, you had to learn fast or pay the consequences. Luckily that learning curve also included some patient teaching. Early on, I was taught a number of things that have served me well. I was a stubborn little cuss and didn't take to all of them at the time, but over the years I've found less and less reason to question their value.

I'm talking about the basics: the little things that many kids no longer learn, and that a lot of adults have forgotten.

The starting point was to respect your elders.
Now that I'm an elderly fart myself, it's no wonder I like this one. I was taught early on not to think I was too big for my britches or down on my luck to say "yes, sir" and "no, ma'am."

I was also taught to show respect to women, and to give respect to those who are less fortunate than you.
When you treat someone with respect, they'll do the same for you.

———

We may have been poor, but my sister, Bobbie, and I were taught to hold our heads up high.

Whether you're young or old, when you meet someone, you look 'em in the eye and speak up so you can be heard. When you look a person in the eye, you're not trying to hide who you are, plus you get a pretty good idea of who they are.

Remembering people's names is the hard part, but it's worth the effort.

When you remember someone's name, they'll always remember you. If you don't know or don't remember their name, then introduce yourself, remind them of your name, and they'll come right back at you with theirs. When these things become habit—a part of who you are—you're on your way to being a person who will make your parents proud.

My parents aren't around anymore, but I know they're watching.

Bobbie and I were raised by my grandmother and, for just a few years, by my grandfather. Our parents were around from time to time, but it was Mama and Daddy Nelson who had the best place for us to grow up, and who taught us things that have stayed with Sister and me, and served us well.

Times were hard in Abbott and most other places during the Depression. We never had enough money, and Bobbie and I started working at an early age to help the family get by. That hard work included picking cotton at age seven in the rows beside Mama Nelson. Picking cotton is hard and painful work, and the most lasting lesson I learned in the fields was that I didn't want to spend my life picking cotton.

Don't be afraid to ask yourself if something sounds right to you.

Sister Bobbie and I were taught to be obedient kids, and to be good Methodists, but not all of the lessons I learned in church sat easy on my mind. In church I was told that if I so much as smoked a cigarette or tasted alcohol, I'd be damned in hell for all eternity. Even when I was a young boy, it didn't take long for me to start thinking that sounded all wrong.

The preacher had sprinkled holy water on my head to save my soul, but apparently that only lasted so long. So at the end of the church service, when the minister asked who needed to be saved, I'd think about the cedar bark I'd smoked that week or the beer I'd tasted, and I'd traipse back up the aisle to be saved from my sins again. It's a wonder I didn't wear out those floorboards.

Even though I sang in the church choir, every time I walked the aisle to be absolved of my sins, I figured everyone in church could see right through me to the truth of my actions. Later I realized it was *me* who saw through who I was and who I was pretending to be.

Using your religion and faith as a guide to your actions will do more for other people than if you just talk about it.

Even as a boy, I didn't cotton to the idea that your religion should be flaunted to other people. Your religion is for you, and is best kept close to your heart.

If you want to know about the lasting influence of my childhood in the church, all you have to do is listen to me sing old-time gospel music like "Lily of the Valley" or "I'll Fly Away." Sister Bobbie and I still play songs from the church in Abbott at every concert, and every few years we record a new gospel album. It's part of who we are, some of the best part.

A song in your heart will take you far.

Maybe the most valuable thing I learned from Grandma Nelson was that you can get through hard times if you've got a song in your heart. I'll be telling you more about my grandmother and growing up in small-town Texas, but for now let me just say that seventy years later—despite all my time on the road—I still think of Abbott, Texas, as my home. I still own a house there, just a hundred yards from where I was born. Seventy years ago, that house was owned by the doctor who delivered me.

Though I've traveled far, my heart hasn't strayed all that far from home.

Them Cotton-picking Nelson Kids 🌿

*My grandmother used to tell me
that a hard head makes a sore ass.*
  —Willie Nelson

I was a hardheaded little cuss, though it's not hard to see why, considering that our grandmother used to wake us in the morning by throwing ice water on us. With chores and work waiting to be done, she didn't have time for coddling sleepyheaded children.

I was red-haired and full of spit and vinegar, so my friends called me Booger Red, which will give you a pretty good idea of my character. Sister Bobbie says when I was a toddler, I was so bent on roaming that Mama Nelson had to stake me out in the backyard on a rope like a wandering goat. I guess I thought there were two ways of looking at things, my way and the wrong way.

We've all heard dads who tell their kids, "It's my way or the highway," but I've been proving 'em all wrong for decades by showing that it's my way AND the highway. Maybe it was singing "I'll Fly Away" in church that gave me the idea of flying away from Abbott, but I used to put on a Superman cape and jump off the roof to prove that I could do it.

When we were three or four years old, Sister and I started going into the cotton fields with Mama Nelson, and before the second grade I was picking cotton myself. We desperately needed the money we could earn picking by the pound, but that didn't make me like it.

It wasn't an easy life, but it was the one I was born into.

Luckily I was also born into a life of music and of the mysteries that surround us.

In our childhoods, we form a bond between ourselves and the great mysteries of the universe. When I was a boy in Abbott, the stars seemed closer, the fireflies shone brighter, and the mockingbirds had yet to hear the car alarms they imitate today. Like everyone else, I grew from a world of magic into a world where the mysteries of creation seem less important.

As we grow up, those mystical bonds we formed begin to slip away. Acquiring reason and practicality, we begin to forget who we were, and often never learn who we truly are.

As adults we try to relax from the never-ending quest for reason and order by drinking a little whiskey, or smoking whatever works for us, but the wisdom isn't in the whiskey or the smoke.

The wisdom is in the moments when the madness slips away and we remember the basics.

Who we were in our childhoods isn't all that different from who we are now.

There's a guy with a lot of lines on his face in my mirror every morning, but the boy from Abbott is there, too. I still love my daddy, Ira, and my mother, Myrtle, and Mom and Dad Nelson, too. I'm as close to Sister Bobbie as when she held me on her knee. I can still hear the songs the black and Mexican workers sang in the cotton fields when we worked, and I still love to sing one of my old favorites, "My Wild Irish Rose."

And every once in a while, it occurs to me that there's no reason why I can't spread my wings and just fly away. Now, where did I put that Superman cape?

> *She is dearer by far*
> *than the world's brightest star,*
> *And I call her my wild Irish Rose.*
> *You may search everywhere,*
> *But none can compare*
> *With my wild Irish Rose.*
> —Chauncey Olcott, "My Wild Irish Rose"

The Willie Way ✍

Let Me Be a Man

Mama and Daddy Nelson gave me a good start on the things that I would come to believe about my place and responsibilities on earth, but those beliefs have grown and deepened over the years.

It took me a while to realize this, but more than anything else, the things you believe in are what make you the person you are.

Since I'm writing a book, it's a lucky thing for me that I put my faith in a number of ideas.

I am a firm believer in the power of positive thinking, and in the wisdom and guidance found in your own heart.

I believe in the eternal cycle of all life that connects us all to one another as well as to the most distant stars in the universe. I believe there is one force that binds the entire universe together, and that force is God.

I also believe that most people have deep religious needs that oftentimes are not met by their church, their synagogue, or their golf pro.

Switching your church or synagogue is easily done, but you're stuck with the golf pro for life.

———

According to the Tao, God is everything and everywhere, and that sounds pretty good to me.

If God is everywhere and in all things, then in stillness and in grace you can talk to God. (Just don't expect God to talk back. Who do you think you are, Moses?)

Speaking of God, did you hear about the priest and the nun who took the afternoon off for golf?

The priest takes a huge swing at the ball, whiffs it, and says, "Shit! I missed."

The nun looks up sharply and says, "Father, you'd better watch your language!"

A couple of holes later, the priest whiffs it again and says, "Shit! I missed."

And the nun says, "Father, God is going to strike you dead if you keep swearing like that."

On the next tee, the priest whiffs it and once again says, "Shit! I missed."

At that moment the sky turns black, the clouds begin to rumble, and a gigantic bolt of lightning comes down and strikes the nun dead in her tracks.

And then a voice from the sky says, "Shit! I missed."

By the way, I do *not* believe in going out into lightning storms after telling jokes like that one.

I believe in reincarnation and the laws of karma, which accrues in our actions, both good and bad.

Nearly all of us believe in science and the laws of nature that science helps us define, but the belief in karma is widespread, though you may think of it the way we used to say it in Abbott:

"What goes around, comes around."

———

I believe in some very old-fashioned ideas called common sense and intuition, both of which make excellent bullshit detectors.

"Once the shit is out of the bull," we say in Texas, *"it's hard to put it back again."*

I believe we are all here for a reason.
And since we cannot truly know that reason, the best approach is to aim high in the manner in which you conduct your life.

I believe that we ignore the law of love at the peril of our own lives and the planet we share.

Above all other things, I believe in the universal truth of the Golden Rule.
Do unto others as we would have them do unto ourselves. Nearly every person on the planet knows this lesson in one form or another.

I believe that creative imagination rules the universe.
I believe in the beauty of first love and the eternal power of all love.
I believe in dreams and in dreamers, being one myself.
I believe in the power of modern medicine and the wisdom of ancient medicine as well.
I also believe in the power of laughter and the beauty of a good joke.

Did you hear the one about the country feller who'd never seen an elephant before? He'd never seen an elephant, never heard

of one, never even seen a picture of one. So an elephant escapes
from the circus, and this guy looks out his window, sees it in his
garden, and calls the cop.

"There's a monster in my backyard!" the feller hollers over
the phone.

"A monster?" says the cop. "What's he look like?"

"He's as big as a house and has a long tail that he's using to
pull up my cabbages."

"What's he doing with the cabbages?" the cop asks.

And the feller says, "You wouldn't believe it if I told you!"

This time I'm confident that there's higher meaning in that
joke. And the meaning is, it's good for you to laugh.

I believe that all life is connected, and that there is beauty
and value in all things.

I believe that the truth is found in your own heart. The
trick is to shut up and listen. The trick is to believe.

I believe in the strength found in being yourself, and don't
give an elephant's ass about trying to fit in or be normal. There
is no normal. There is only you and me.

I believe in me and in you, and trust that you do the same.

Picking Up the Tempo 🎵

Music is a vibration.
  —Confucius

There were two kinds of culture in Abbott when I was a boy—one was agriculture and the other was yogurt.

Luckily, Sister Bobbie and I were born into a world of music. We had a house full of music books and Mama Nelson taught Bobbie to play the piano and to read music. After I got my first guitar at age six—a Stella that came from the Sears & Roebuck catalog—I'd sit on the end of the bench and play along with her.

Our daddy, Ira, was a fine guitar player, and an even finer auto mechanic. Our mother, Myrtle, was a singer and dancer, and as free a spirit as ever came out of Texas. Because Ira and Myrtle each needed different things, they divorced when I was just six months old, but both continued to be a positive influence on our lives.

There was music in our Methodist church, of course, and more music coming from the Baptist and Catholic churches, and the Church of Christ, which had no instruments.

The voices of the choir were all they needed to make beautiful music.

When we picked cotton, we were accompanied throughout the day by farmworkers whose music lived deep in their hearts. When I turned on the radio, I heard stations from Chicago to the Mexican border playing everything from Ernest Tubb and Bob Wills to

Bing Crosby, Tommy Dorsey, and—when I was ten years old—a new young singer named Frank Sinatra.

I didn't care for music lessons, but Bobbie covered my ass by learning music theory backwards and forwards while I went adventuring, and she's been covering my ass ever since with her playing and her knowledge of music.

When we were five or six years old, our grandparents put Sister and me on stage and said, "Our kids do things. Now start doing."

We've been doing ever since.

I was in the sixth grade when I got my first paying music gig, strumming guitar in the John Raycheck Band in Bohemian dance halls. Mama Nelson was dead set against me working in sinful nightclubs until she found out I could make eight or ten dollars a night. You had to pick a lot of cotton to make eight dollars.

Music has been my life, and will continue to be as long as I am able to hit a lick on the guitar and find the voice that lives inside of me, just as strong today as when Dad Nelson put that first three-dollar guitar in my hand and showed me how to make a C chord.

Sister Bobbie and I both have perfect pitch, which means our grandparents taught us to reproduce the memory of how many vibrations per second were passing though the tunnels between our ears.

Music is a vibration, and words are airwaves. Music and words in unison are harmony.

A life in the way of the Tao means living in harmony with the world and those who inhabit it. Sharing that harmony has taught me so much, and it all started with the musical home I was born into back in Abbott.

The Golden Rule ⌇

Heaven is eternal, earth everlasting.
—The *Tao Te Ching*

Some people like to make a big deal about their particular religion. If your religion is an important part of your life, then I am happy for you without any regard for which religion it is.

As far as different religions are concerned, to me they're just different paths leading to the same place. A thousand paths to a single destination.

The Golden Rule is the main thing I live by, and every religion I've read about or studied—both East and West—has the Golden Rule as a common thread running through it.

Every person is free to believe whatever the heck they want to believe, but if every person, every business, and every government simply followed the Golden Rule in all their decisions, everything else would just fall into place.

Do unto others as you would have them do unto you.

Unfortunately, we don't always like things to be so simple. We like to talk about infinite shades of gray when the simple truth is right before us in black and white.

Do unto others as you would have them do unto you.

———

In many Eastern traditions, the phrase translates with un-canny accuracy. The world according to Confucius says the guid-ance for your goodness of heart can basically be summed up as *"Do unto others what you wish for yourself."* Sound familiar?

With the Christian and Jewish faiths, it all goes back to Abra-ham and the Old Testament. It was Abraham who said, "Don't screw with me, Jack, and I won't screw with you." (Okay, he may not have used those words exactly, but that was the gist of it.)

We used to see the Texas version of that in the old Red Ryder Western movies when Wild Bill Elliott would say, "I'm a peaceful guy, and I don't want any trouble." Then they'd mess with him and he'd wind up killing about thirty of them. He tried to tell 'em, but they just wouldn't listen.

You can get a pretty good idea of the type of kid I was by my "Booger Red" nickname. There was a definite pecking order in Abbott, and if you were on the bottom of it, you had to fight for your place against every kid all the way up the ladder. The only way to avoid that fate was to pick the toughest kid and challenge him to a knock-down, drag-out pissing, moaning, and ass-kicking match that involved everything from bare fists to rolling around in the rocks, dirt, and stickers till one of you turned tail and ran.

It wasn't a pretty sight, but if you gave as good as you got, in the long run you didn't get quite so much.

Times have changed of course, and as individuals we've man-aged to put most of that kind of behavior behind us. As nations, however, we still have a long ways to go. As nations, we are par-ticularly fond of the idea of many shades of gray.

As nations, we prepare much more for war than we do for peace, and in doing so, we make war inevitable. Achieving peace through strength doesn't necessarily mean that you need bigger tanks or missiles, for peace can also be achieved through personal strength.

No matter the rationalization, any destructive act leads to other destructive acts. One kid punches and the other kid punches back, and the only way it ends is for the kids to grow up and realize that you can actually get in the last lick by taking it, not by giving it.

Just because we were taught the Golden Rule as kids doesn't mean it doesn't apply to us as adults, or as nations.

As much as I admire the nonviolent message of Gandhi, in the practical world, the Golden Rule ultimately provides reason in situations where nonviolence leaves some tough alternatives. After all, I am only a man, and doubt that my belief in nonviolence would restrain my human reaction if you mess with my family.

The practical advantage of the Golden Rule over a philosophy of total nonviolence is that by admitting the likelihood of response in the case of an attack by an individual or a nation, you are not left in a defenseless position. The greatest power is one you do not have to use.

The beauty of the Golden Rule is that it applies to so many situations. Even in a peaceful world . . . if we ever get there.

The Willie Way ✍

The Cowboy Way

It's true. My heroes have *always been cowboys.*

Since the earliest days of the Old West, when a cowboy's life depended on his horse and his amigos, the cowboy way has been a profound and practical guide to doing things in a way that would make your mama proud. The cowboy way springs from common sense and from a strong sense of right and wrong, without regard for consequences.

In the long run, the cowboy way believes that if you do things according to that sense of right, it'll work out to everyone's advantage.

If you do things that try to make sense out of wrong, all kinds of bad shit can result. For starters, you may get yourself killed off or sent to the hoosegow—both very negative incentives that should help keep you from screwing up.

Besides, every time you act from the wrong motives, people you know and who rely upon you lose respect for you. And respect is not something that you can just buy back.

The respect of others must be earned through the positive qualities of our actions.

In the fifties when he played Davy Crockett, Fess Parker became a Texas and American hero through the way he personified the strength of Davy's beliefs and actions. Davy's motto in the Fess Parker Disney films was, "Be sure you're right, and then go ahead." Even if you think it's corny, that phrase still makes sense.

People and nations moving ahead when they're wrong is the root of many of the world's problems.

At the beginning of this book, I wrote that if you love music, you are my friend. But I neglected to mention that there are also exceptions that stand in the way of friendship and brotherhood.

If you throw trash along the highways or foul our rivers, I'm sorry to say you are not my friend.

If you think that people whose skin is a different color from yours are beneath you, then you are particularly not my friend.

Nearly forty years ago, I introduced country singer Charley Pride to a redneck audience that looked like they wanted to lynch him for being black. Before they knew what was what, I'd walked up to Charley and kissed him full on the lips. The crowd was so shocked, they actually quieted down and listened to his music and discovered that he was pretty dang great.

In other words, they got over their wasteful and ignorant prejudice. If you haven't gotten over yours, you are somewhere between forty and four hundred years behind the times.

You'll never get ahead by blaming your problems on other people.

Now where was I? Oh, yeah . . .

If you mistreat those who are smaller or weaker than you,
you are not my friend.

If you use the knowledge you've gained to exploit others,
you are no one's friend (and run the risk of having no true
friends at all).

The life I value is one that is connected to all things. The
secret to happiness lies in finding those connections. You are
the road and the river; you are a paintbox of colors but are
only learning how to use them; you are not as strong as you
feel, nor as smart as you think. Most of us have too high an
opinion of ourselves anyway.

Whether you call it the cowboy way or the way of the Tao,
open your heart and you will be as strong as the strongest
among us, as wise as the oldest sage. Open your heart and you
will share the joys of every perfect game, taste the bounty of
every plentiful harvest, and feel the pain of every mother who
loses a son at war, whether from your country or from the country they call your enemy.

With an open heart, you will see the grace in every falling
leaf, and taste the life contained in every drop of rain. The
trick is not to be afraid of the beauty or the rain.

There comes a time in each of our lives when we have
the opportunity to reach out and turn the switch that will
change darkness to light. All we have to do is slow down, remember who we are and who we would like to be.

All we have to do is make those connections to our fellow
man and to the world around us. Then we have to reach out
and turn on that switch.

I can't tell you where the switch is, or when you might be

able to find it; I can't guarantee that it will work the first or the second or even the third time that you try it. I just know it's there, waiting for you.

I'm just an old cowboy poet, a song singer on the road of life. I don't know as much as I could, but I do know that if you've come this far with me, then you are my friend.

And I hope that each of us finds our way.

Cherokee Nation ✒

*In the old days our people had no education. All their wisdom
and knowledge came to them from dreams. They tested their
dreams and in that way learned their own strength.*
  —Ojibwa elder

From the wild Injun kid to the ponytailed, peace-pipe smoking
chief of the Nelson clan, I've never doubted that my Indian blood
is a big part of who I am. My grandmother Bertha Greenhaw was
three-quarters Cherokee Indian and her husband was half Cherokee and half Irish. I guess that means that I can't be trusted with a
bottle of Irish whiskey and a scalping knife.

The Cherokee people—or the Tsalagi, as they referred to
themselves—originally occupied a large portion of the Allegheny
Mountains. Forming friendships and forging alliances with the white
settlers who came into their lands, in just a few decades the Cherokee saw their homelands become Virginia, Tennessee, the Carolinas,
and much of Alabama and Georgia. In none of those states, sadly,
was there room left for the Tsalagi.

The religion of the Cherokees—like most Native American
tribes—is a mix of zootheism, or animal worship, combined with
the worship of all tangible things including the sun, the moon,
and the stars. The sun and moon, for example, were considered to
be sister and brother. Humans were thought to be the sun's grand-
children and the younger brothers of the moon. With belief in
gods above and below the earth, in the waters and across the land,

the Cherokee seemed to share much with the way of the Tao, which also sees God in all of creation.

Despite their written language and their long support of the U.S. government, in 1838 and 1839, twenty thousand Cherokee were evicted from their homes and forcibly marched west on what would soon be known as the Trail of Tears. Already adapted to the world of white men and ill-equipped for a winter journey on a wild frontier, four thousand Tsalagi men, women, and children died of starvation, exposure, and disease along the way.

This is one of the most shameful chapters in American history and serves as a strong reminder as to why we should never allow our ambitions for America to blind us to the possibility of misguided action on the part of the government. Those in power should never be confused with the documents and law that grant them that power. Being elected or appointed does not necessarily make you right. Following the letter of the law and the universal truths in our heart is what makes something right.

Knowing that my ancestors got a raw deal, I've long believed in supporting American Indian causes. My appearances at various Indian events over the decades have made me closer to my Indian heritage and helped me to understand more about who I am, and why I think the way I do.

In 1987, I was named Indian of the Year in Anadarko, Oklahoma, and spent all night playing music and dancing with fifteen thousand Indians. That experience made it clear to me just how powerfully musical Indians are, and what a large influence my Indian blood has been on my music.

All Tsalagi music was thought to have begun with the slaying of a monster named Stone Coat, a living rock who was protected by his stone coat. As the Tsalagi defeated the monster with a huge fire, the Cherokee people were witness to songs and dances that sprung from their burning adversary. Passed down through countless generations, these songs and dances helped bring success in war and in the hunt, and were used as a medicine for treating sickness.

Perhaps that's why I believe so strongly in the healing and nurturing power of music.

One of my favorite Cherokee stories speaks as well to us today as it did to the Tsalagi hundreds of years ago.

The Tsalagi believed that within each person was a battle between two wolves. Sitting with his grandson, a grandfather explained that one of the wolves was evil and was driven by anger, envy, regret, ego, and the worship of war.

The other wolf was good, and was driven by love, hope, compassion, and the promise of peace.

Thinking about the wolves already growing within him, the boy asked, "Grandfather, which wolf wins?"

And the old man replied, "The one you feed."

The Willie Way 🍃

Breathe

When I was very young and just learning music, my grandmother taught me that voice control depended on breathing from way down deep. Through deep breathing, you strengthen your lungs, your vocal chords, and every other part of your body, including your heart.

People tell me they're surprised that I don't run out of breath at my concerts, even when I sing for a couple of hours straight. When the all-day golf game swings into an all-night poker game, my pals are amazed that I'm able to keep going at all. I don't explain it to them, but I will to you. The secret is breathing.

Everyone knows that filling your lungs with oxygen is good, but not many people choose to do it.

This is like most of the choices you have in life. You know inside whether it's right. Whether you do it is up to you.

Deep breathing can work wonders for your physical, mental, and emotional state. Simply by breathing, you can bring divine energy into your lungs, and through your blood to your heart and your mind.

Breathing is its own form of meditation. Breathing can calm you and put you in touch with your own spirit. If you concentrate and listen to your own breathing, what you will hear is the sound of God.

I've been the butt of plenty of jokes about deep breathing my Austin torpedoes, but even I'll admit that deep breathing fresh air is the most natural high.

Breathe from your chest; breathe from your gut; breathe from your heels.

Through breathing, you deepen your contact with the world around you. An open window is a wonderful place to breathe deeply. When you clear your lungs, you expel the old and take in the new. The new air, of course, brings oxygen to your lungs, your bloodstream, and all the cells of your body, including your brain. When you expel the old air, you also provide carbon dioxide for trees and plants that make oxygen for you.

The logic of the circle of life is to plant a tree and breathe deep.

The hardest thing to see on this incredible planet is the eternal circle of life, which is anchored by the links between sky and water, between day and night, winter and summer, O_2 and CO_2. Each of those links is infinitely more solid and everlasting than you and me. The water we drink, the food we eat, and the air we breathe are our connections to that circle.

We have many forms of spiritual strength, but physically the choices are few and simple. If the choice you make is to breathe deeply, you can uncork the genie of your own personal power.

Crazy 🖎

The Wisdom of the Pigs

Worry
Why do I let myself worry
wondring
what in the world did I do?

I'm crazy
for thinking that my love could hold you
I'm crazy for crying
I'm crazy for trying
I'm crazy for loving you.
　　　　—Willie Nelson, "Crazy"

My life was a little uneven after I ventured from Abbott into what I thought of as the real world. I joined the Air Force but was discharged with a bad back, and soon after returning to Abbott, I married Martha Jewel Mathews. Martha was a sixteen-year-old full-blooded Cherokee maiden, and every night at our house was like Custer's Last Stand.

For the next decade, I chased the dream of country music stardom, but also worked as a disc jockey, teaching guitar, and a whole lot of other jobs. Three kids with Martha, followed by a second marriage to singer Shirley Collie, was the kind of thing that would have settled a lot of restless souls, but not me.

By the early sixties, I'd made enough of a mark in Nashville to swell my head like a ripe watermelon, but had also known enough frustration to make me wonder if I was ever going to fit in. Faron Young had recorded my song "Hello Walls," Billy Walker had recorded "Funny How Time Slips Away," and Patsy Cline had recorded "Crazy." All three songs had been big hits. I'd also recorded my own records and toured with singer Ray Price and his band, the Cherokee Cowboys, but success at singing my own songs was hard to come by.

I was pretty good at making money during the sixties, and even better at spending it. Beating my head against the Nashville music business taught me some valuable lessons, and so did my wayward attempt at raising pigs on a farm outside of Nashville.

In the music business, I learned that clothes do not make the man.

I tried to fit in by looking the way they wanted me to look, and I just didn't look like me. I also tried to sound the way they wanted me to sound, and I didn't sound like me either.

Speaking of which, what do a record exec and a sperm have in common?

Give up? They both have a one-in-a-million chance of becoming a human being.

Though I recorded a lot of albums for Liberty, Monument, and RCA records, none of them made me a big Nashville star. I was also not much of a pig farmer. The pigs had a great time, but I didn't make any money at all. Whether farming or otherwise, I was learning that life is simpler when you plow around the stump.

I also learned that you should never name a pig you plan to eat. Especially if you've got kids.

———

I learned some other invaluable lessons in Nashville that apply to both farming and show business.

Do not corner something that you know is meaner than you.

Keep skunks of all kinds at a distance.

And I learned:

If you forgive your enemies, it messes up their heads.

I never met a pig or a record executive worth holding a grudge over anyway.

Instead of holding a grudge against them pigs, for thirty years, I've been getting even with them one bacon sandwich at a time.

As for the record executives, I did my best to be patient, and eventually found several that I actually like. The reward for my patience has been that 250 albums after I started, I'm beginning to think I've got the hang of this business.

I read somewhere recently that I've sold 50 million albums, and that's not counting all the bootlegs and a whole lot of independent records that don't get counted. The same story said I rank tenth on the all-time list of artists with the most gold, platinum, and multi-platinum albums. My total of twenty-four is just behind Dylan. If we keep touring together, maybe we can pass Frank Sinatra, who is just ahead of both of us.

If we don't, it's nice to be in Frank's neighborhood.

The lesson I've learned is, don't give up if you know what you're doing is good.

And that doesn't just apply to music.

Don't Think No Negative Thoughts ✎

Either that wallpaper goes, or I do.
—Oscar Wilde's final words

While I was fighting and often failing to find success in Nashville, I became a champion of negative thinking, and that had made me a self-destructive SOB. After Dad Nelson died when I was seven years old, I'd started writing cheating songs even though I wasn't old enough at the time to know what I was talking about.

By the time I hit my thirties, I'd been married twice and knew plenty about relationships gone wrong. I was still writing lots of cheating and heartbreak songs, and that got me thinking that's the way life was supposed to be.

Life is not about how fast you run or how high you climb, but how well you bounce. Unfortunately I was hitting so hard that I didn't have much spring to my rebound.

I've always had my own way of singing, and it was nothing like the way other Nashville stars sang. It really bothered me that nobody else thought I could sing back then, and all that negative thinking was one of the reasons I'd been divorced and had my share of scuffles in bars. My head was just pointed the wrong way . . . which reminds me of a not-very-funny joke.

———

A guy goes to the library and asks for books on suicide. The librarian sends him to the shelves, but he soon comes back and says, "There's only two books."

And the librarian says, "They never bring them back."

I figured I was too smart for a book on the subject. One night I got so down on myself that I lay down in the middle of the street in front of Tootsie's Orchid Lounge in Nashville and waited for a car to come by and run me over. If I lay down in that street today, I wouldn't be so lucky, 'cause there's a lot more cars there now, but downtown Nashville moved pretty slow at night back then. When no cars came along for quite a while, it occurred to me that there was no one to blame for this sorry situation other than myself. Once I realized I was the culprit in all the shit that had gone wrong in my life, I also realized that eventually it'd all turn out okay.

In a flash, I started to believe that—just as I'd visualized myself as hard-bit and brokenhearted, then seen that come to pass—I could visualize myself in ways that I truly wanted to be and make that come to pass. I was like a drunk that quit drinking. I developed a real positive attitude toward my own life.

It's not easy to live positively in a world that thrives on the negative, but I turned myself around and made it known that I didn't want people bringing their negative shit around me. Maybe I don't write as good of cheating songs as I used to, but that's a small price to pay for what I've gained. It took me a long time to realize that I didn't have to make life so danged hard.

Because of positive thinking, there is very little that I've wanted to do that I haven't been able to do.

———

I've written more songs that I ever dreamed possible, and I've also learned not to panic when the next song takes a little time to arrive. When I couldn't write a song, Roger Miller used to tell me, "Don't worry about it. When the well runs dry you have to wait a while for it fill up again."

So when I'm not writing, I figure whatever I'm doing is filling up the well.

I also enjoy making movies and would like to make a few more good ones like *Barbarosa*, *Wag the Dog*, and *The Dukes of Hazzard*. Just working to make that happen is a satisfaction all its own. One big reason I'm liable to have the opportunity to make more movies is that I truly believe it will happen. The power of my confidence and enthusiasm is a good deal of what will make it come to pass.

On the other hand, when you live in a circle of negative thinking, when you are petty and selfish, when you use your handful of money or power to dominate others, you are already living in a hell of your own making.

If you've made your own hell, then only you hold the power to escape it.

It is up to you to spread life and spirit through the positive, not the negative, to be generous and to think of others as of equal importance as yourself, to use whatever money and power you have to make the world a better place.

If that sounds corny and quaintly old-fashioned, then ask yourself this: What truly would the world be like if everyone lived their lives in the most positive way possible?

Of course, I may be dreaming, but what the hell, I figure we might as well dream big.

Home to Texas 🖋

If English was good enough for Jesus Christ,
it ought to be good enough for the children of Texas.
> —Ma Ferguson,
> former governor of Texas

Life is a quest for returning to God.
> —Kahlil Gibran

The end of a hard decade in Nashville slammed shut when my house burned down. So I moved to Bandera, Texas, and started getting my head right. I read Kahlil Gibran's *The Prophet* and Edgar Cayce's books about reincarnation, and I got into the teachings of Father Taliaferro of St. Alcuin's Community Church in Dallas. I also started playing golf regularly and began to meditate, occasionally at the same time.

In *The Prophet*, Gibran wrote, "Your heart knows in silence the secrets of the days and the nights. But your ears thirst for the sound of your heart's knowledge."

Learn what you already know in your heart—that sounded pretty good to me.

Edgar Cayce believed that Earth is a living library for all the rest of the universe, and that every person on the earth carries the record of that history in their genes, their blood, and their bones.

And that made sense to me. Earth and everything on it is

formed from the same matter that comprises the stars and everything else in the universe. Every member of the human species links back to earliest man, and whatever changes that have occurred along the way are seen in one way—by looking at ourselves today.

Nature has chosen your form. What you do with that form is up to you.

If you could do anything, what would it be? If you could grow wings and fly to the moon, feed a thousand hungry children, or simply play beautiful music, what would you choose?

Only you can know your own heart.

Father Taliaferro was an inspirational teacher who founded the nondenominational Saint Alcuin's Community Church in Dallas. The patron of Father Taliaferro's church was Saint Alcuin, an educational and religious scholar who is often credited with spawning the Renaissance, during which Europe emerged from the Middle Ages.

It was Father Taliaferro who helped me see that creative imagination rules the universe.

Father Taliaferro believed that you must "learn that you may teach."

Whether it was due to these inspirational teachings, to my positive attitude, or just to good timing, suddenly a lot of good things started to happen for me. All through the sixties, I'd built up a good following in the old Texas dance halls like Randy's Rodeo in San Antonio, Panther Hall in Fort Worth, and the Broken Spoke in Austin. These places felt like pure-D old-timey Texas, and the crowds were a lot like the folks I'd grown up with in Abbott.

But suddenly I began to find new audiences as well. Or perhaps they found me. One of the principal places this happened was in Austin at a cosmic new concert hall called Armadillo World Headquarters. The Armadillo was nothing fancy, but the beer was cold and the jalapeños on the nachos were hot, and the audiences— who were a wild mix of cowboys and hippies—liked all kinds of music.

I had so much fun playing for the Armadillo audience that I brought Waylon Jennings down from Nashville to play for them, too. Waylon took one look at that crowd and said, "Willie, what kind of shit have you got me into?"

But they loved him. Austinites in the seventies were partial to good music, and they still are today. That's a big part of how the music show *Austin City Limits* could thrive for thirty years.

One of the Armadillo's regular performers was a spiritual teacher named Ram Dass who used to pack the place like he was a rock star. Ram Dass used to say that you could acquire knowledge— which is rarely a bad thing—but you could not acquire wisdom.

"You can't know wisdom," said Ram Dass. "Wisdom, you have to 'be.' "

Somewhere on the path to "being" wisdom, one thing I learned is that the mind, rather than being the master, should be the servant of the heart.

Finding a piece of my heart staking claim to Austin, I made up my mind to call the place home. Life was good, and I was about to make some of the best music of my life.

The Willie Way 🐛

Cool Water

A guy goes to the doctor complaining that he doesn't feel well. The doc checks him out, then gives him three bottles of pills.

"Take the blue one twice a day with a big glass of water," says the doctor. *"Take the red one three times a day with a big glass of water, and take the green one four times a day with a big glass of water."*

"Oh my God!" the patient says. "What's wrong with me?"

And the doctor says, "You're not drinking enough water."

Life and water are inseparable. Three quarters of the earth's surface is covered by water, just as three quarters of your body is made up of water. Even in the driest desert where rain may come just once every few years, the cycles of life are based on waiting for the arrival of water. Our bodies are not so patient.

Every cell in your body needs water to survive, and that means that drinking plenty of clean, fresh water can make you stronger, healthier, and smarter. Water carries oxygen and fuel to your cells, lubricates your joints, regulates your body temperature, and plays a key role in just about every function of your body.

My number one roadie, Poodie, says, *"You can't make a turd without grease."*

I like the line, but the truth is, what your turds need is water, because a lack of water in your body will result in everything from constipation, dry skin, and headaches to urinary infections, blood clots, and strokes. Every time you breathe, eat, or smear some product on your skin, toxins accumulate in your body. Water flushes those toxins away.

Though we know we're supposed to drink six to eight cups of water a day, most of us still don't do it. The average American drinks more sodas and beer than he does water. The sodas have massive amounts of sugar, which cause obesity and diabetes, or artificial sweeteners, which just plain scare me. The beer tastes good on a hot day but, like all alcohol, is a diuretic and removes water from your cells rather than replenishing it. Got a hangover? It's because you've both poisoned and dehydrated your cells.

The average American consumes over fifty gallons of carbonated soft drinks a year. One can of soda contains ten teaspoons of sugar—ten! If you're battling your weight, get rid of the sodas. I'm not trying to put the soft drink companies out of business, but the bottom line is, you should drink water when you're thirsty, not sugar, alcohol, and caffeine.

In Austin in the eighties, because we were having way too much fun and suffered the price, about once a year we'd go on a diet where you drank water mixed with cayenne pepper and a little lemon juice. The idea was to flush the toxins we'd ingested through a lot of hard living. It seemed like a good idea at the time, but as I stood pissing firey water, eventually I realized it was smarter to be careful about what I ate and drank in the first place, and by making sure I drank enough water.

For most of us in America, clean water is easy to come by. All you have to do to is make the choice to get it to your mouth.

Piss more; you'll live longer.

The Night Life 🖎

When the evenin' sun goes down
You will find me hangin' 'round
Oh, the night life, it ain't no good life
But it's my life.
     —Willie Nelson, "Night Life"

Scuffling around as a young man looking for a way to get ahead, I landed in Fort Worth, where I played dance halls on Saturday night and taught Sunday school the next morning.

Church folks like to have a good time, too, so I used to sing "Amazing Grace" on Sunday morning to some of the same people who'd heard me sing "Whiskey River" on Saturday night. I didn't have any problem with that, and neither did they.

The minister at the church, unfortunately, couldn't see the beauty of this arrangement. Maybe he wasn't aware that contradiction exists in all of us. Or maybe I hadn't connected to him the way I had with his congregation.

Much of life can be summed up as connecting with other people. You may accomplish that with an easy smile, by being a good friend, or by lending a hand when you can. Maybe you do it through all of those and more. Someone repeatedly saying they're your friend is not nearly so convincing as repeated displays of friendship.

In all things, your actions do speak louder than words.

———

My show is about connecting to the audience.

When I walk out onstage, the first thing I do is start searching for a friendly face. Once I make a connection with that person, the energy we've created starts bouncing around to others in the room, and building up so that pretty soon the whole place is lit up like a neon sign. When the audience, the band, and I get to that point, we could keep going till dawn, but it all starts with that first friendly face.

In a good show—and to me they're pretty much all good shows or else I wouldn't keep doing them—in a good show, the audience and I lift each other up. We put each other on a natural high.

When a performer opens his heart to an audience, he shares his deepest feelings with them. An audience doesn't want to find a big bank vault hoping to fill up with their money, they want to find love in a performer's heart.

Those connections we make end up leading all of us to a better place—a place where thousands of people join in and sing along on both "Whiskey River" and "Amazing Grace." So, not that much has changed since the honky-tonk and Sunday-school days fifty years ago.

Most of the members of my family band have been playing with me for over thirty years. No one has an exact tally as to the number of shows we've put on, but it might be in the neighborhood of ten thousand. We've played everything from two-bit shit holes to 100,000-seat stadiums, and maybe twenty million people have heard me sing with my family band.

Even after all those shows, it feels good to be out there playing with family for all our friends. As I mentioned earlier, we've got a lot of friends. I'm still knocked out by all the people at the show, and the mix of the crowd is part of what I like best about it. We get lots of young people, plus we get lots of older folks who have been listening to my music for a long time.

The last couple of summers, we've been touring minor-league baseball parks with Bob Dylan. That keeps us out of the corporate amphitheaters and it brings a lot of families to the shows. The best part is that kids under twelve get in free. How great is that? When I look out there and see three or four generations from one family boogying and bebopping to the music, the good feelings I get make the long drive to tomorrow night's show a hundred miles shorter. At least that's the way it feels.

Gator and L.C. may be driving the bus, but it's the audiences that move it down the highway.

So when people ask why I still go out there and sing every night that I can, the answer is simple. Because I enjoy it. I've got the audience I've always dreamed of, and I like playing music with the greatest musicians in the world. Add it up, and the result is I get entertained every night my ownself.

Besides, if I'm not out there on the concert stage, I'm probably picking for free at Poodie's in Austin, so I might as well do it where I'll get paid. Otherwise I might have to teach Sunday school for a living.

Songwriter ✍

I knew someday that you would fly away
for love's the greatest healer to be found.
So leave me . . . if you need to . . .
I will still remember . . .
Angel flying too close to the ground.
> —Willie Nelson, "Angel Flying Too Close to the Ground"

Ask me a dumb question like "What's the secret to writing a good song?" and I'm liable to give you a wiseacre response like, "It's the lyrics and the melody."

Sarcasm aside, the truth is that besides those first music lessons, my grandmother taught me music was anything that's pleasing to the ear. After I learned that, I didn't think about it much more.

For Sister Bobbie and me, learning perfect pitch wasn't nearly as complicated as it seems. Your eyes and brain learn the frequency of the colors that we commonly refer to as blue or red, and with some innate musical talent and a little practice, your ears and brain can learn the frequency of C or B and a lot of steps in between.

I've also heard it said that perfect pitch is when you throw a banjo in the trash and it hits an accordion.

Toss in a snare drum and that joke would make its own rim shot.

Speaking of squeeze boxes, an all-accordion band plays a New Year's Eve gig. After the show, the manager says, "Not bad, boys.

Can you play next New Year's?" And the band members say, "Great. Can we leave our instruments?"

The deeper meaning, in case you didn't get it, is that all-accordion bands don't get a lot of work.

I've never written any tunes for the accordion, but I have penned around 2,500 songs. One result of all that writing is that I'm not quite as motivated as I used to be and don't feel like I have to write any time in particular. Now, instead of searching my brain for the songs, I just let the songs come to me. And I'm thankful when they do.

The Tao teaches that the act of creation is a form of liberation. You can't always change the circumstances of your life, but you can change your perception of those circumstances and of the world around you by any creative act.

Remember Father Taliaferro. Creation will set you free.

So to each of you, I say, "Create!" It doesn't matter what: a line of poetry, a phrase of a song, or a perfect pot roast.

Cook a perfect pot roast and you will never dine alone.

If it's songwriting in particular that you're interested in, here's a bit of what works for me.

In Nashville, we were taught that the shorter you can make a song and still get your point across, the better the chances of airplay.

My bunch of songwriter buddies—like Roger Miller and Kris Kristofferson—were taught to say what you wanted to say in six or nine lines of verse or whatever was gonna fit. That helped us concentrate on the lines we wanted to use and forced us to put more thought into them. I'd sooner have three great verses than thirty mediocre ones; if nothing else, it makes the song easier to remember.

———

Whether short or long, good songs are timeless; you can do 'em to-day or a hundred years from now. They're still good.

Texas songwriter Ray Wylie Hubbard says that the most important question to ask yourself after you write a song is, "Can I happily sing this song every day for the next thirty years?"

In the seventies, Hubbard wrote "Up Against the Wall, Redneck Mother," and his crowds have howled for it at every show he's done since. Of course, Ray Wylie does admit that going to the mailbox twice a year to get the royalty checks has helped ease the burden of singing it over and over and over . . . and over.

So it's a good thing I really like singing "On the Road Again," 'cause I often launch into it two or three times a night. It's just a great song to keep the crowd up and moving forward with us.

The other thing about writing a really good song is that you'd better be prepared for thirty years of people interpreting what you meant in that song.

Different songs often mean different things to different people.

"Angel Flying Too Close to the Ground," for instance, is one of my favorite songs, and it's one that's inspired great passion. Many members of the Hells Angels, for instance, feel certain that "Angel Flying Too Close to the Ground" is about one of their members who died. Now, I'd be the last person to tell a big group of kick-ass bikers that they're wrong. As far as I'm concerned, whatever they feel the song means is just fine.

Theirs is far from the only interpretation of the song, and I make it a point not to disagree with any of the interpretations (as long as you're not trying to sell your junk food or your god or your war with my song).

It's not up to me to tell you what my songs mean.

The meaning is already in the song. And the song is *the meaning.*

"Angel Flying Too Close to the Ground" IS the Tao of Willie. It and a whole bunch of other songs I've written are the reflection of what I've learned on a really great ride on the merry-go-round called Earth.

And if the ride keeps going for a while longer, I may learn more, and thereby cast a bigger reflection. So keep the wheel turning, I say. And keep your angels flying high.

Blue Skies ☙

Those who know others are wise, those who know themselves are enlightened.
  —The *Tao Te Ching*

Though I didn't move back to Texas to boost my career, when I got back home to Texas and back to who I was, my career began to take off in all directions. I could try to shuck and jive you about the way I'd planned it all out, but the truth is, when I got my heart in the right place, my career followed along.

Back in Texas, it was easier to remember all that great Mexican and Spanish guitar pickin' I'd heard as a boy, and those sounds helped fill out two albums I made for Atlantic Records. *Shotgun Willie* and *Phases and Stages* were both hits, and I followed those with *Red-Headed Stranger*, a concept album that told the story of a frontier preacher who'd been wronged by his wife and another man.

A couple of albums later, I was selling records like hotcakes when I decided to do a collection of standards called *Stardust*. I'd just become famous for being a long-haired outlaw, and the record execs didn't want nothing to do with a bunch of forty-year-old songs like "Stardust" and "Blue Skies."

Of course, when the album stayed on the charts for ten years—and eventually sold ten million copies—they wanted to know how I found all those great old songs.

But I didn't find them—those songs found me, and they did it over the airwaves when I was a boy listening to the music of Hoagy Carmichael and Bing Crosby late into the night.

I'd never forgotten "Blue Skies," but it wasn't till I got back to Texas that I realized they really were smiling down on me.

Scientists tell us that the sky is blue because our atmosphere refracts all the colors except blue back into space. They may well be right, but I believe the sky is blue because blue is the nature of the sky.

Everything in creation must be true unto itself. Each bird can only fly according to its own nature. If a bird decides in mid-flight to fly in a different way, the results are not gonna be good. A hummingbird cannot glide high on thermal winds, and a hawk cannot hover in front of a tiny flower.

If it's in your nature to stay constantly on the go—as it is mine—then you have to keep moving or else you will fall.

According to the Tao and to a lot of people throughout history who managed to find what they were looking for, happiness comes from being true to your true nature. It's mainly by trying to be something else that people go wrong.

If you are a good person, if you have a good heart, you don't have to be nothing but yourself.

One of the reasons I've survived in music is that, no matter what kind of music I'm singing, my own style rings through. While Turk and I are writing this book, my reggae album, *Countryman*, is just being released. And I can tell you in all honesty that *Countryman* is my favorite album . . . until the next one comes out. In the meantime, I'm number one on the reggae charts. *Jah Rule!*

I'll probably have released several more albums by the time this book appears, which is the kind of thing that drives record execs crazy. The whole music business is built around the model of releasing one gigantic album every couple of years, while my idea is to play as much music with as many great musicians while I can.

Which do you think I should choose—big business or more music?

When you look at your life with the proper perspective, the choices are surprisingly easy. When you ask the right question, the answers aren't so tough.

Musicians with their own styles—like Johnny Cash, Waylon Jennings, and Ray Charles—are the ones whose careers last a lifetime, and whose popularity lasts well beyond their lifetimes. When you heard Johnny Cash on the radio, you knew it was the man in black. He didn't try to be anything other than himself.

The same thing went for the King of Texas Swing, Mr. Bob Wills, from whom I learned so much. When I was thirteen years old, I sang a duet with Bob Wills, who was always happy to let someone sing or play the lead fiddle parts instead of him. Whoever was singing, Bob Wills knew who he was, and who the audience came to see.

In the end, all that we can know is ourselves and the tiny part of the world around us.

I've always loved morning glories, those lovely flowering vines that open their blossoms with the morning light. A morning glory knows nothing of the night. By day, the mystical, twinkling firefly is only a flying bug. Though they are connected by place, they are separated by time and know nothing of each other. In their own way, each is a mystery.

The Tao teaches that people of deep spirit breathe the wind

and drink the morning dew. You may think that's crazy, but I like the way it sounds, and prefer to appreciate life's mysteries and trust in its truths.

If you want to make great music or just have good friends, you have to get your heart right.

Follow your own guidance and you will never be alone. Trust your own truths, and blue skies will follow wherever you go.

The Willie Way 🕊

Meditation

When I need to get in sync with my inner thoughts, I've found that meditation is one of the best ways to do it. If you've never tried meditation, no worries, because it's really about *not* trying. It's about just being. On the other hand, a few key words might help get you started and keep you focused.

Sit. Listen. Breathe. Dream. Renew.

Sit.

Sit still and quiet. Relax your muscles, your eyes, and your mind.

Listen.

Listen to the sound of your own breath and to the wind, the earth's breath of life. Listen to the movement of the leaves on the ground or in the trees, to a mockingbird, a dove, or a distant train. In the country a rooster crows. In the city, laughter.

All the sounds blend into one, then fade away.

If you sit quietly enough, you will hear and feel the beating of your heart.

Breathe.

Let your mind flow away like a river without beginning or end, like the waves rolling up and down the shore. You are part of that river. You are one with the ocean, with the wind. You are the bird and the leaves; you are your thoughts, your words, your breath. You are alive.

In this distant quiet, there are no bills to pay, no papers to shuffle, no rules to obey, no bad deeds to regret, no wrongs to right, no good left undone. In this moment, worry has been replaced by contentment, confusion by understanding, fear by courage, agitation by calm.

Dream.

In your dream, you may stand outside your body, then walk around yourself in a circle. Smile.

In this place, there is no fear of other people or their ways, for in this place, there is no difference between you and them.

What is this mysterious and magical place to which you have journeyed?

This place is you. This place is a remembering of the miracle of your own life.

Renew.

When you come back to the thoughts of your body, to hunger and thirst, to responsibilities and destinations, all you need do is remember to take a part of this simpler you on your journey through the world.

Now you're on the road again, making music with your friends. I've always found that it's good to get back on the road again.

The Second Mouse ✎

The early bird may get the worm,
but the second mouse gets the cheese.
—motto on Willie's coffeemaker

Question for you: What were the redneck's last words?
"Hey! Watch this!"

That's a good one. Considering all the stupid things we do in life, we should probably keep in mind that there is no lifeguard in the shallow end of the gene pool.

So far, I've survived all of my stupid mistakes—and there have been plenty of them—but rather than dwell on them as negatives, I like to think of them as learning experiences that will hopefully keep me from killing myself off prematurely or otherwise screwing the pooch.

Short of learning by trial and error—and don't you wonder who was the first guy to jump out of a plane strapped to a device that would one day function as a parachute—there are better ways to learn.

The fact is, wisdom is all around us, even as stupidity abounds.
The trick is to be open to one without succumbing to the other.

As my friend Harry Anderson says, "It's important to keep an open mind, but not so open that your brains fall out."

While I grew up playing music, Harry grew up learning magic and playing around with the idea of being a con man. After he fleeced a few score of sheep on the street with his three-shell game, it took just one encounter with an irate sucker for Harry to realize that ripping people off was not nearly as wise a play as showing them how *not* to get ripped off.

The slight shift from being a con man to pretending to be a con man opened all kinds of doors, and Harry soon graduated to the much bigger con of getting himself cast as the lead of the hit sitcom called *Night Court*. Ask him about it today and Harry says, "I was very big in the eighties."

The only hitch was that after leading the number one show in America, and after fifteen years in television, Harry realized he liked being a magician better than being a TV star.

So he shucked it all and went back to his roots. Having lopped a zero or three off his income so he could run a little magic shop in the French Quarter of New Orleans, Harry is either incredibly wise or pretty darn stupid. I'll leave it to him to figure out which, but I do know that with or without a big pile of money, he's still Harry. Without his magic, I'm not sure we could say the same thing.

Harry showed me a great trick the last time the band and I were in the Big Easy. First he borrowed a twenty-dollar bill from me; then he tore it up, burned the pieces, and vanished the ashes. When I asked him what happened to my twenty, he said, "The money is always there. It's just the pockets that change."

He also had a joke, which was worth just about twenty bucks.

A guy is on his deathbed, with his wife at his side. Racked with guilt, the man takes his wife's hand and says, "I have a confession."

But his wife says, "No, no. It doesn't matter."

"I have to confess," he says. "I slept with your sister . . . and your best friend . . . and your mother."

And his wife says, "I know. That's why I poisoned you."

The Willie Way 🕊

Let It Go

The funny thing about advice is that no matter how good it is, most people are gonna do what they want anyway. That's why my general philosophy has been never to miss an opportunity to shut up. So now that I'm writing a book in which I'm constantly giving advice, I must remind you to read the warning label on my bottle of wisdom.

Because something works for me doesn't mean it will for you, especially in large doses.

When a doctor prescribes a medicine, he doesn't suggest you take the whole bottle, and neither does my part-time gynecologist alter ego, Doctor Booger Nelson.

Speaking of Doctor Nelson, did you hear about the woman who was such a fan of country music that she has a tattoo of Merle Haggard done in a very delicate spot, high on her right thigh, and a tattoo of Waylon Jennings high on the other thigh.

Worried that the two tattoos weren't recognizable, she slips off her undies, lifts her skirt to a guy in a bar, and says, "Can you tell who that is?"

So the guy puts on his glasses, looks real close, and says, "I don't know who those other two guys are, but the one in the middle is Willie Nelson!"

That's a good one! But if you're suddenly pissed off over the crude nature of that joke, all I can say is, it's not a perfect world, and sometimes you just have to let your anger go.

In trying to observe people who pass through my life—or who just pass by in traffic—I've noticed that most people spend too much time worrying about what someone else is doing or saying.

If you're peeved about the guy who cut in front of you or the ass kisser at work who got promoted, those thoughts are likely to bounce around in your noggin for hours or days at a time. And the result of that will be that you're no longer a little peeved. Instead you'll be a whole LOT peeved, or seriously *pissed off*, as it's called in the polite society I hang around in.

Now if you want to go through life pissed off about traffic and jackasses, that's your own business, but do so at the risk of not noticing the other driver who kindly let you in when your lane ended, and all the good folks at work who help make your job a little easier.

I could have gotten all pissed off thirty-something years ago when my wife Shirley tied my drunk ass to the bed with a clothesline and woke me up by beating me with a mop handle, but instead I figured I probably had it coming. Thinking back on it now, I realize I *definitely* had it coming.

Instead of letting your thoughts think you into a corner, why not just let them go? Letting go of your anger by simply exhaling it away makes room for the ultimate breath of fresh air.

If someone's a jerk, that's their misfortune, not yours.

Let the jerks of the world serve as the perfect example of what you *don't* want to be. You'll be a heck of a lot happier, and in the long run, there's a chance that other person at work will end up asking what your secret is. Why are you the happy one?

In other words, don't let your thoughts think you.

Besides, if you're really gonna get pissed, don't waste it on your family, friends, or coworkers, save it for something that really matters.

The problems of the world are many and large, so if you're gonna get pissed, it ought to be about hungry children, or the fact that health care is too damned expensive and illiteracy too prevalent. It might do some good if more people were angry about the unjust sharing of power and decision making in politics and business, about family farmers who suffer so corporations can thrive, or the general living, medical, and education standards for the five and a half billion people on earth who've got a much tougher life than you and me.

One of the great benefits of helping people who are less fortunate than you is that it gives you a new perspective on your own life. Appreciate what you have and you'll be in a better frame of mind to make the world a better place for those who have less.

That may not change other people's driving habits, but when some jackass cuts you off, chances are you won't give a shit anymore.

And that'll probably really piss him off.

Just Play It ✍

Those who know do not say.
Those who say do not know.
    —The *Tao Te Ching*

You can't kiss a duck's butt
without getting feathers on your mouth.
    —The Tao Texas Ching

No matter how old you are, your life is a time-limited offer. It's possible that you've been here before or will be back in another life, but in this life, the two most impossible things to change are the time you are born and the inevitability of your passing.

While all the miracles of modern medicine can't eliminate the physical limits of the human body, there is no limit to what you can learn.

Over two thousand years ago, the masters of the Tao taught that while life is finite, knowledge is infinite.

Knowledge is a tricky thing. Unlike a big business deal, you can't sign a paper that will bring you a large sum of knowledge. Knowledge can only be acquired by learning, which must be done on a day-to-day basis.

But what is knowledge? And what good is it once you've got it?

After sixty-five years of playing, I know quite a bit about playing guitar. I have good technique, some of it taught to me by my old friend Paul Buskirk so that I could reteach those same lessons to students at Paul's school of guitar.

But I don't play guitar by technique. I just play.

I guess you could say that I play by something beyond technique. You might call it feel, but the Tao calls it the Way. Skill and technique can enable you to do a thing well and in exactly the same way each time. But doing something according to the Way will enable you to do something that is different each time, and which is also great.

I don't play the same notes each time, I play the song, and the song plays me. We are the same.

You don't need to play guitar for these thoughts to apply to you. You can do good things in your life—like helping a little old lady across the street—or you can forget the technique of doing good and let the good things simply be a part of you.

Whether playing guitar or simply trying to be a good person, if you are constantly guided by your intellect and by techniques that you've learned, you will likely be concerned about how good you sounded. Your motivation will be in trying to achieve success.

We are all pleased by success, but if you do things the way they come natural to you, you'll be more than pleased—you'll be satisfied.

Happiness is in the way we act, not in the outcome.

One of the secrets to my sound is almost beyond explanation. My battered old Martin guitar, Trigger, has the greatest tone I've ever heard from a guitar—and I've played a lot of guitars, including a lot of other Martins that were the exact same model as Trigger.

A lot of the guys in the band have been with me for decades, but Trigger has outlasted every musician I've played with, and after all these years, I have come to believe we were fated for each other.

The two of us even look alike. My musician pals haven't carved and written their names on me the way they have on Trigger, but we're both pretty bruised and battered.

The holes I've worn in Trigger are from my pick zinging up and down a million times on the face of an acoustic guitar that's not supposed to be played with a pick, but at this point those holes are part of what makes Trigger sound exactly right.

I also play other guitars, of course, including a black electric Fender during the blues numbers on our show, but Trigger is as much a part of my sound as the way I play.

If I picked the finest guitar made this year and tried to play my solos exactly the way you heard them on the radio or even at last night's show, I'd always be a copy of myself and we'd all end up bored. But if I play the instrument that is now a part of me, and do it according to the way that feels right for me—in each place and time—then I'll always be an original.

At the very least, I know it won't get bored.

Live in the Present ✒

I live one day at a time
I dream one dream at a time
Yesterday's dead and tomorrow is blind
and I live one day at a time.
  —Willie Nelson, "One Day at a Time"

I feel pretty happy right now. I'm on the bus rolling through the Rocky Mountains, and I'm drinking a cup of coffee and listening to some classic country music on the Hank's Place channel on XM Satellite Radio. I guess you could say there's no place I'd rather be.

If you consider all the people you know who seem truly happy, there is likely to be one trait—one essential perspective on life—that each of these happy people shares. Some people have to learn this and some just seem to know it instinctively, but once this knowledge is truly a part of you, I don't believe that it can be taken away.

What is the incredible secret? It is the word now. *It is the understanding that happiness exists at just one time. And that time is now.*

You may have BEEN happy yesterday morning, and you can BE happy about how yesterday turned out, but you can't BE happy yesterday. You can only BE happy today, this hour, this minute . . . *now.*

Did you get there? Were you happy? I hope so, but if not, it's too late, that moment is gone. But wait, here's another one. Are you happy now?

Since life is a journey, let's think of it as a road trip. Ahead of you are untold opportunities for joy, learning, sharing, and a lot of fantastic sunsets and sunrises. And every one of these opportunities will be at the intersection of your trip and a road called Now.

Unlike a real highway, it's not a problem if you doze off and coast right through the corner of Now and Happiness avenues, because life is an infinite progression of these intersections, and each of them holds opportunity, surprise, and the promise of a smile.

But if you're asleep at the wheel your whole life, you're gonna miss a lot of places called Now.

Thousands of pages and millions of words have been written about living in the moment, but it is not a complicated idea. All you have to do is open your eyes—and all your senses—to the world around you.

The easiest mistake on earth is to forget to appreciate what you have right now.

Take last year, for instance, when my hand started knotting up on me and I found it almost impossible to play guitar. I went to see a bunch of doctors and they got worried looks on their faces, and that put a worried look on my face, and that got my band and crew looking really worried. When I don't work, they don't work. And we all like to work.

So I had to take a few months off for surgery. And while my hand was healing more slowly than I wanted it to, I had a lot of time to appreciate all those gigs that I'd sometimes let myself think were just the okay gigs.

Away from the road, I realized that every show is a blessing.

I'm not trying to say that nothing goes wrong in my life. Or in yours. Your love life may not be perfect—okay, chances are your love life is definitely NOT perfect. Work may leave something lacking, and you may be a few coins shy of that Jamaican vacation you've been dreaming about. But those are not causes of unhappiness. Those are distractions, obstacles, and challenges to overcome.

You may carry a big chip on your shoulder about things that happened to you in the past, but that chip is nothing but a weight that's anchoring you to intersections you've already passed. Quit looking in the rearview mirror and set your sights on the road ahead.

Not long before Ray Charles passed on, I was at his birthday party in New York City. Ray and I had been close for a long time, and we loved being together, whether it was playing music or chess. The first time we played chess, Ray sat me down in the dark at a Braille chessboard and he just kicked my ass. After that, I said when we played chess, we had to have some lights on.

After Ray's birthday party, we went over to the Apollo Theater in Harlem for the anniversary of the theater and I sang "I Can't Stop Loving You" in tribute to Ray.

We were talking later that night and Ray told me, "Willie, there are a lot of younger people than you and I already gone on. So it has nothing to do with age. There's those huge disasters that happen on the planet when thousands of people get wiped out, and that has nothing to do with age either. One way or another, we're all headed that way."

So yeah, Ray, we're all headed that way. And the next time you and I get together, we can play one more game of chess without the lights.

Ray Charles was a man who lived in the moment. Ray knew how to let go of the burdens of his past and enjoy the good things he found in the present.

Let go, and you'll be free to find happiness now. And the best part of that is that once you learn to do it, you can do it again and again and again, until it becomes instinctive.

Start with a technique—the technique of happiness—and you will eventually progress from skill to mastery. If you master happiness as the art of now, there will be times in your life— perhaps many of them—when you and happiness will have merged into one.

You and the Way will be one and the same. You'll be on the road. You will BE the road. Right now, I'm the highway from Denver to Durango, and for the moment, there is no other road I'd rather be.

Like they say, you've got to slow down and smell the flowers. Or in my case, smoke the flowers.

The Time of the Preacher 🎵

The red-headed stranger had eyes like the thunder,
And his lips, they were sad and tight.
His little lost love lay asleep on the hillside,
And his heart was heavy as night.
    —Willie Nelson, "The Red-Headed Stranger"

Anything that is not a mystery, I like to say, is guesswork. From the reason you are here to the understanding of the golf swing, there is so much you can never know.

Over the years, I've done plenty of singing in church, but I've played just one preacher, the lead role in the film *The Red-Headed Stranger*. The story of a preacher in the Old West who'd been betrayed by the woman he loves, the red-headed stranger loses his way in revenge, but ultimately finds redemption by gaining love again.

Whether we know it or not, we are all in search of understanding.

Religion, science, art—all of them are devoted to a greater understanding of the mystery of life. How the mystery of life affects you is really your own choice. To you, that mystery may be the source of fear. Or it may be your well of inspiration.

Many fine people find comfort in their religious beliefs or just a strong faith in God. So let me ask you a simple question. What is God's religion?

While science has given us a greater understanding of the

universe, our concept of God is relatively unchanging. To most of us in Western culture, God is a wise old man who listens to our prayers and controls our fates. But to think of God as looking like us and as a fixer of our problems seems like a self-centered way to view both God and the universe.

A lot of other, equally fine folks place their faith in simply trying to be good human beings. Does this mean God disapproves of their lives?

It's impossible to know if one of these approaches is right on, or even if one is more right than the other. If we *knew*, life would not be a mystery.

The way I see it, different religions are just different paths leading to the same place.

If you look around, you'll see we have a long ways to go before we get there, but the path to God is clear. Whether you're a Southern Baptist or an Eastern Buddhist, if you think of God as everything in the universe, including you and me, then your ultimate responsibility is to live your life in harmony with God. That doesn't mean the teachings of the Old Testament or the Zen masters don't apply; it means that our ultimate responsibility is toward the good of all. All. That's me and you, and everyone else.

To be a servant of God, we must love unselfishly. When everyone is able to do that, then we will have found heaven right here on earth.

Because there is one God in all things, there exists a fundamental level at which all things are one, where I am you and you are me. One religion or faith may be right for you, another for someone else. But in the long run, what matters more are not our differences in beliefs, but the beliefs we share.

All of us care about our own welfare, about our families and friends, our countries and our fellow men and women as a whole. And when every person on earth admits that and acts along those lines, we won't need any more advice from old cowboy preachers or just about anyone else.

It's really so simple, and it all comes down to love.

Family Man 🪶

It's a dream come true.
There is nothing that a dream can't do.
I dreamed of love and I was given you.
You're a dream come true.
— Willie Nelson, "Dream Come True"

If the idea of love seems to leave out too much of the mystery and too little room for miracles, perhaps you're failing to see the obvious.

Miracles are all around us.

You want miracles? Then look around you. If you are a parent, your own kids are a miracle. That doesn't mean that your kids don't sometimes act spoiled and ungrateful, or make fun of how clueless their parents are.

But in the craziness of trying to raise children in a crazy world, most of us forget that our children were conceived in one of the ultimate acts of love, that they somehow grow from a tiny fertilized egg into a complete human being that is perhaps the greatest wonder of the universe.

Just like you, your children are made of atoms that started in the big bang that created the universe.

When you are gone, if things work out according to nature's best plans, your children will be among the last people on earth that have a direct memory of who you were. They'll sing your praises—or not—depending on how you raise 'em up, and the kind of guidance, love, and friendship you give them.

And if you do well for them, your children will ultimately take care of you in your final weeks, months, or years.

Sprung from all creation to be a precious and irreplaceable part of your life—how can that not be a miracle?

I'm never far from my family. Sister Bobbie is there with me on the bus and onstage playing piano every night. My daughter Lana is also on the bus, working the computers and posting the Perdenales Poo Poo, the daily account and pictures of our life on the road, on my Web site, WillieNelson.com. Check it out.

Annie and I have been married for nearly twenty years now, and she used to be with me on the road all the time. Our boys were conceived on the road. They came into the world and started growing, and after a few years, they needed to stay home and in school, while I needed to be on the road. They weren't too crazy about the arrangement and neither was I, but patience is bringing us back to where we started, because now we spend a lot of time on the road together.

We'd need a lot of buses if all my family traveled with me, but they don't have to be on the road for me to appreciate them and the good parts they've played in my life.

The older I get, the more I realize it's never too early to start appreciating the people in your life.

If you love your family, it's essential that you tell them. They need you and you need them.

If you can make someone feel better with just a few words, why wouldn't you want to use them?

Speaking for fathers everywhere, this is the best I can offer.
Go hug your daddy. It ain't too late to save him.

What Would Willie Do? ⚡

When I don't know
how I'll get through,
I ask myself, what would Willie do?
　　—Bruce Robison, "What Would Willie Do?"

Austin songwriter Bruce Robison's song "What Would Willie Do?" is about a guy who guides himself through tough decisions in life by asking what I'd do in the same situation. It's a fine song—and funny, too—and I hope the sentiment helps Bruce in the tough choices he has to make. (He already married the lovely and talented Kelly Willis and they've got kids all around, so he seems to be doing okay so far.)

The best part of having a song written about my so-called wisdom is that I can play it for people when they give me any shit. But where does that song leave me, I'm often asked, when I'm looking for someone's advice to follow?

Over the years, I've learned that I have the perfect person to steer me as well. When I'm contemplating one of life's difficult decisions, I generally consult with the world's oldest living roadie, Ben Dorcey. Once John Wayne's personal valet, Ben is now eighty-one, but doesn't look a day over eighty-one and a half.

Bless his barely thumping heart, Ben is my canary in the coal mine. So when faced with a difficult decision, I generally observe Ben and do the *opposite* of what he does. If Ben orders chicken, I order fish. If Ben wants mayonnaise, I want mustard. If Ben wants a window, I want the aisle. If Ben says use two rolling papers, I use three.

So the best advice I can give you is, don't be like Ben. One Ben Dorcey is perfect, but the world doesn't need another.

The purpose of life is not merely to serve as a warning to others.

And that reminds me of a joke.

Question: How come Hitler didn't drink?

Answer: 'Cause it made him mean.

Since there's not much to be learned from a crazy asshole like Hitler, the rest of us have to find more positive examples of what we really need. When I'm looking for positive guidance, I think I just try to consider who I am and what is the right decision for me. As with breathing deeply or drinking plenty of water, there are a lot of simple choices in life.

You know inside whether it's right. But you still have to choose to do it.

The way I see it, if you start out looking at somebody, wondering whether they're good or bad, you've already started in the wrong direction.

We're all good and bad, and the only difference is in our actions and our words.

Besides, cruelty is all out of ignorance. If you knew what was in store for you, you wouldn't hurt anybody, because whatever you do comes back more forcefully than you send it out.

The Willie Way ✎

Things I've Had to Learn Twice

They say the success of a rain dance is generally related to its timing. I suspect that the success of advice-giving works pretty much the same way. So if any of the following things I've learned does good things for you, I'm happy to take credit. If not, then I say we blame it on the weather.

There's too much and too little.
That's a good metaphor for a lot of things, but I'll leave it to you to figure out what they are.

Above all things, patience.
The best freedom is the ability to control your own life. That's something you don't achieve just once, but over and over and over again.

We are all pure potentiality. The question is, for what?

I believe that all roads lead to the same place—and that is wherever all roads lead to.

Make your choice and stick with it. . . . No, wait, that's not it . . . but it could be, I guess. Is it too late to change my mind?

———

There's nothing wrong with saying no . . . unless you're married.

There's nothing wrong with saying yes . . . unless you're married.

There's nothing wrong with saying what you believe . . . unless you believe some pretty weird shit, in which case you may want to keep your trap shut.

If you want to find something, stop looking. If you already found it, stop looking. If you forgot what you're looking for, stop looking.

But if a pretty girl goes by, look.

If a frog had wings . . . it would get bird pussy.

If you don't own stock, you don't have to worry about how you're doing in the great Wall Street gamble.

It's important to recognize the difference between want and need.

In the consumer-driven world, most of us sense that possessions won't bring us happiness, but still find it almost impossible to want less. So don't fill up your life with crap, especially a bunch of cheap crap.

No matter what you do, be truthful.

No matter how hard you try, you cannot force a smile.

Guy Clark had it figgered out when he wrote "Stuff That Works."

There's a lot to be said for an old Buck knife that'll keep

its edge, a bus that'll always get you to the gig, and a guitar that sounds just as good today as it did forty years ago.

Sammy Allred had it all figgered out when he declared a five-dollar fine for whining.

Ray Benson had it ALL figgered out—I mean the whole shebang—but then he realized he was just stoned.

Clean living and dirty thoughts are not mutually exclusive.

Farmers work the hardest. Waitresses are second. Hookers get an honorable mention.

I'm not a farmer or a hooker, but I like myself better when I'm writing regularly and working hard.

I'm no doctor, but it's not hard to see that one of the chief causes of high blood pressure is worrying about the possibility of high blood pressure.

Pushing your luck does not count as exercise.

Ninety-nine percent of the world's lovers are not with their first choice. That's what makes the jukebox play.

Most of the stuff I've read about me has been true.
I'm not a know-it-all, but I'm beginning to know myself.

Funny is all around us, but you have to let it in.
There's nothing better for your mind and body than a great laugh—except for great sex, of course, but let's face it, a good laugh is a lot easier to find, plus you don't have to buy someone a house when you get caught telling the joke to another woman.

———

People used to ask one of my ex–fathers-in-law for advice, and he'd say, "Take my advice, and do what you want to." So that's my advice. . . . Listen to the voice that comes from your heart, then do what you want to do. It's worked so far for me.

And finally, a good memory is the most important . . . I'm sorry, I forgot what I was going to say.

Fortunately We Are Not in Control 〜

We wake up in a new world every day,
And we wouldn't have it any other way.
　　　　—Willie Nelson, "Wouldn't Have It Any Other Way"

"Don't sweat the small stuff" is one of the best pieces of advice I've heard. Or is it *"Don't pet the sweaty stuff"*—I never can remember which.

Confused?

Join the club.

Does it sometimes seem as if you have no real say in what happens in your life?

There may be a good reason for that.

Do you feel like the years are racing by like fence posts outside your car window, and you've misplaced the steering wheel?

There's a good reason for that, because you are careening out of control, flying through the universe at a million miles an hour. AND THERE'S NO BRAKES!

Let me guess: now you're *really* confused. Am I talking about your life or the cosmos? To be honest, I'm a little too confused to say. But here's the good news.

A certain amount of confusion is inevitable in life. Every day— possibly every hour—we are all faced with a thousand decisions.

What to eat? What to say? Where to go? When to stay? Why do this? Why not do that?

As I say to the band, indecision may or may not be our problem.

I'm sure your life is also plenty complicated, but since I don't know about yours, pretend for a moment that you're me. This year, like just about every year, you'll travel tens of thousands of miles in the company of four or five buses, several semi-trailers of equipment, a large band, an even larger assortment of friends, family members, roadies, technicians, and various assorted hangers-on. All of this will be scheduled around a couple hundred audiences, each of which numbers in the thousands, and it all has to happen on time or everything will fall apart.

Each night, I have to decide which songs to sing and in what order, and the only thing that's certain is that we'll run out of time or the venue will run out of beer before I run out of songs.

So things tend to get a little complicated—as things tend to do—and the most single important thing for you to remember is not to panic.

When the panic—among other things—hits the fan, there's one key phrase to remember:

Fortunately we are not in control.

Sounds so good, I think I'll try it again.

Fortunately we are not in control.

There. I feel better already.

"Fortunately we are not in control" is my way of saying it ain't my fault, and probably isn't anyone else's fault either.

So if we're not in control, you're probably wondering who *is* in control. And the answer is: I don't know. But it ain't me, and it ain't you, because . . .

Fortunately we are not in control.

———

Here's the good part. Once you admit that you can't control everything, then it becomes clear that sometimes you just have to let things happen. It just makes everything so much easier, and it keeps you a lot happier with the way things work out.

Think of it this way:

If you get out of bed thinking everything's gonna be wonderful, all too soon you're going to see things happen that aren't so wonderful. And if you walk around thinking everything's going to be terrible, then you're gonna obsess on that and miss what was good.

So where does that leave us?

An excellent question, because we are left with the simple fact that the beauty of life is in the discovery of things *as* they happen.

Like my first wife, Martha, used to say, "Don't worry about a thing . . . there ain't nothing gonna work out right."

I'm not sure I knew what she meant at the time, but she seemed happy when she said it.

Sixty years ago, if I'd had the opportunity to lay out my whole life just the way I wanted it to happen—whatever I would have planned would have paled in comparison with what's actually happened.

And all I can say about that is . . . Fortunately, I wasn't in control.

The Willie Way 🖎

Nothing I Can Do About It Now

A couple has been married so long that the wife can't remember the last time they had sex. So she goes to the lingerie store and tells the clerk she wants to buy the sexiest, most expensive lingerie in the store.

The clerk shows her a sheer slip of a thing and says that it costs $500. But the woman says she wants something sexier and more expensive, so the clerk finds an almost transparent negligee that costs $600.

When she wants something finer still, the clerk says the garment on the hanger he's holding is so transparent, it is almost invisible.

The woman buys the invisible nightie, takes it home, and says to her grumpy old husband, "I've got a surprise for you. I went lingerie shopping."

She goes into the bathroom to change into the nonexistent negligee, then walks out to show it off for him.

"This is the most beautiful negligee in town," she says. "And it costs $800."

And the husband says, "For $800, you'd think they could have ironed it."

Damn, I'll bet he regretted saying that! But once something has been said, it cannot be unsaid, *especially* in a marriage.

In marriage and elsewhere, there's an easy way to avoid regret:

Keep your words sweet. You may have to eat them.

Regret is a funny thing. When allowed to rise, it occupies time that might be devoted to something constructive. When left alone, it lurks in the corner just waiting to be fed. I'm not going to pretend for a moment that I haven't screwed things up plenty in my life. But the older I've gotten, the more I've come to believe in my own songs:

> *I know just what I'd change*
> *If I went back in time somehow*
> *But there's nothing I can do about it now.*

They say that whether you're extracting wisdom or wisdom teeth, you have to pull hard and it may hurt down deep. Understanding regret has been one of the hardest lessons there is.

I used to blame myself for things that had gone wrong in my life, but eventually I had to set myself free of what might have been. Eventually I realized that I was the only one who could set me free.

I am the only person who can set myself free from what might have been.

The Man in the Mirror ✎

Who knows his own nature knows heaven. So what is our true self? That is the central question.
  —Sankara

Just about every one of us develops a pretty good bullshit detector. If you haven't got a clue when you're being shucked or jived, chances are you don't have five dollars to show for the past year of hard work you've put in.

But for some reason, that same skill for detecting other people's bullshit doesn't seem to detect our own. I mean, you're reading my advice—and you hope it's good advice—but let's be real, how can you know for certain? Maybe I'm just full of it.

At some level, I suspect we're all full of it. It's hard to go through life without a little gloss of bluster and bullshit to dazzle the lambs and keep the wolves at bay. That's probably not a bad idea, especially if you're fond of lamb and fear the wolf, but you also have to remember one of life's most important lessons.

Don't be dazzled by your own bullshit.

Unless you're a true master, who you are and who you pretend to be are two different things. They say clothes make the man, but those same clothes that make you more of one type of man make you less of the other. So which one are you, really? Are you the clothes? Or are you the man?

I like putting on a tux and braiding my hair for a special occasion like the Kennedy Center Honors, where Gator drove the bus right onto the stage for me to receive my award, or at the Texas Medal of Arts awards, where they hung one around my neck and said so many nice things I almost forgot who they were talking about.

I could spend a good deal of my time listening to people talk about what a pure-D musical genius I am, but that don't get the songs sung or the people dancing. No matter how many nice things they say, I'm still a picker and a songwriter and a dad and grand-dad, and a fair-to-middling dominoes player.

Beyond the basics of who you are, the rest is mostly creative use of adjectives.

Luckily, I've got a good bullshit detector with me at all times on the bus, and I suspect you've got one at home as well. It's called a mirror.

If I need a reminder about who I am or who I'm pretending to be, all I've got to do is look in the mirror and ask if that's still me. If the answer is yes, then I'm on the right track. But if I look in the mirror and see someone else, then it may be time for some changes.

You might want to do the same thing from time to time. Go on, give yourself a long, hard look in the mirror. After you get past "Damn, I look old!"—look a little closer. Look between the lines, if you will. Look at the shape of your smile and the glint in your eyes. Is it you, or is it a mask that you wear for other people?

If you don't see you, keep looking until you do. You're in there somewhere. When you've located yourself, stay there a bit longer.

Lean back and watch yourself take a deep breath. That breath means you're still alive. You don't know nothing about tomorrow, but today you're still ticking. Today is a blessing. You may not have noticed, but trust me, it is.

We'd probably all be a lot happier if we'd just remember how lucky we are to be alive on this beautiful planet.

So you're standing in front of the mirror, the masks are falling away, and you're breathing deep, from all the way down at your heels.

Now look closer, peer into your eyes. Are you there? Do you see yourself as a child who trembled at the lightning but always counted the seconds till the thunder? Who knew the magic of fireflies on a summer night, and the satisfaction of your mother's or grandmother's home cooking? If you let those things go, a part of you will go with them.

In my mirror, I may see the moment that I'd finished writing "Family Bible," and known that I'd done good. In my eyes—and yeah, in my lined face, I see my kids at every age—good times and bad, happiness and sorrow, they're all there, their lives are a part of me, and I will never let that go.

If I look long enough and deep enough, I see that the boy from Abbott is the same as the old man on the road. That the grandson I was is still a big part of the grandfather I am. I see that I'm lucky to have a place in the world, lucky to have people to love and people who love me. Lucky to be alive and to have a song to sing, and another to sing after that one.

My family, my friends, my music, and my willingness to just be me have made me strong and carried me far. They are the happiness in my heart.

When I'm true to myself, that helps me stay true to them as well. They may not always see it that way, because I'm sure there are plenty of times that each of them would like me to stay a little closer to home.

But I hope that eventually they'll understand me and understand themselves as well. Even when I'm far away, they're all with me. Especially when I look in the mirror.

You may have to bullshit your way past strangers every once in a while, but there's no lying to family. Or to yourself.

It's easy to be false with other people, but to be false to yourself is a waste of your life on earth. Look in the mirror. Live.

Free Willie! ✐

Our life is our own possession,
and its benefit to us is very great.
  —Yang Chu,
    early Taoist teacher

Have you heard the story of the University of Oklahoma research program in which a female chimpanzee named Washoe was taught to communicate by sign language? After years of patient instruction, Washoe had learned 140 signs relating to her and the immediate world around her. Obviously this was one smart chimpanzee.

So after learning 140 signs, Washoe finally advanced to the point that her teacher thought she might be able to express her own feelings. Washoe, by the way, had been treated with respect her whole life, and she'd known nothing but good living conditions. Despite the comfortable circumstances of her life, when encouraged to express her feelings, what Washoe said over and over again was, "Let me out!"

Like all of the rest of us, Washoe wanted to be free.

In ancient times, there was a deep dispute between the beliefs of the Tao—which remain difficult to even put into words and must ultimately be understood through intuition—and the later teachings of Confucius, which are easy enough to grasp that they still fit nicely on a slip of paper inside a fortune cookie.

Confucius had some fine insights, but also taught that the individual should conform to the norm of accepted moral standards and duties. The only problem with that is that someone has to decide what's normal. And there goes your freedom.

The way of the Tao, on the other hand, trusts that a moral guide exists within your true self.

Trying to make a country music success of myself, I spent plenty of time trying to be normal. I wore suits that didn't suit me. I sang songs that didn't sing to me. And I went along with other people's choices instead of making my own.

I still made a lot of good music, but more important, I learned a valuable lesson. What I learned is that I'm not normal.

Think about it—do you know even a single person who's normal? Chances are, you think *you* are the most normal person in your entire circle of family, friends, and coworkers. I mean, face it, isn't there something just a little strange about every dang one of them? They're just not normal.

There is no normal. There's only you and me.

So if I'm not normal and you're not normal and *they're* not normal—why in the blue blazes do we all spend so much time pretending we are?

Why would any of us want to change our natural way of living just to be pleasing to someone else?

Yang Chu, the fellow I quoted at the beginning of this chapter, lived 2,500 years ago, and even then he wrote at length about maintaining what is genuine in your life and in the world around you, about the basic need for freedom, and about ways to maintain that freedom in an increasingly complicated and encumbering world.

Just because his thoughts have been handed down to us from the ancient traditions of China does not make them Chinese. These thoughts have circled the globe a thousand times and even found their way into our Declaration of Independence and Bill of Rights. They are no more Chinese than I am. But they are timeless.

The North Star knows the way of the Tao and never veers from its course. The sun and moon have it and never come to rest.

If each of us were as true to ourselves as the North Star, then we'd have the same guidance in our lives that ancient mariners had when they ventured across uncharted seas.

There is only one map to the journey of life, and it lives within your heart.

Money Man 🎵

Willie has no respect for money;
that's why his cash is all wadded up.
    —Poodie Locke

To know you have enough is to be rich.
    —The *Tao Te Ching*

On first glance, you might conclude that I may not be good with money. But if you look closer, you'll realize that I'm *definitely* not good with money.

From where I started—dirt poor in Abbott and working everywhere from the cotton fields to the school cafeteria to bring in some money—you'd think I'd have learned the value of the stuff. Maybe I'm just a slow learner.

After Daddy Nelson died, we moved from our two-story home to a house that wasn't much more than a shack. I'd lay in bed at night, look at the stars through the cracks in the ceiling, and dream of making a success of myself and bringing in lots and lots of money.

In the meantime, during the day, I hocked my guitar so much, the pawnbroker could play it better than me.

Remember my first paying music gig with the John Raycheck Band? It was a big band and there was no way the audience could hear twelve-year-old me strumming my acoustic guitar, but maybe

I got the gig because it looked good to have a plucky kid up there on stage. Or maybe I just made Mr. Raycheck look tall.

I wasn't always so lucky, and did a lot of scuffling for money in the next twenty years.

In the fifties, I sold the rights to some of my best songs like "Family Bible" and "Night Life." My daughter Lana was little when I sold "Family Bible" for fifty bucks, and she says it broke her heart for me to let something go that was so close to our family. I've been asked a thousand times how I could sell a great song for fifty bucks, and the answer is pretty simple. I really needed fifty bucks.

And that reminds me . . . a dapper guy is sitting at a bar listening to a woman lounge singer and notices that the man next to him is sobbing in his beer. "Hey, buddy," the dapper guy says, "why the tears?"

And the sobbing guy says, "That singer is so beautiful . . . I'd pay a hundred dollars just to touch her breasts!"

That perks up Mr. Dapper, who says, "I'm going to take that as a compliment, because that singer is my wife." Just then, she finishes her set and walks over to the bar. The dapper husband says, "Honey, this gentleman is crying because you're so beautiful. He says he'd pay a hundred dollars just to touch your breasts."

"That'll be the easiest hundred bucks I ever earned," the wife says. And with that, she lifts her blouse over her head, exposing her breasts. But when she looks up, the man is sobbing louder than ever.

"Now what's wrong?" she asks.

And the man moans, "I haven't got a hundred dollars!"

Nearly thirty years after I sold "Night Life" for fifty dollars, I was fairly confident that I'd put my scuffling days behind me. I owned a golf course, a recording studio, and an assortment of houses and ranches, and I didn't ever have to worry about where the next dollar was going to come from. Then one day I answered the phone and discovered that I owed the IRS sixteen million dollars. Shortly after that, the debt magically became thirty-two million.

Money is a funny thing. No matter how high you stack it or where you hide it or invest it, they can still take it away from you.

So here I was, an eight-dollar-a-day guitar player from Abbott, Texas, who the IRS claimed owed them thirty-two million bucks, which might have been more than I'd made in my whole life. This happened not because I was trying to cheat our government, but because I'd taken the advice of financial advisors who were supposed to be the best in the business. Stupid me. (And here's the funny part. I knew the advice sounded kind of fishy in the first place, but I hadn't followed my own instinct.)

In no time, my studio, golf course, and ranches were taken away from me, and it seemed as though—no matter how long I lived—I'd never be able to repay the debt. But even though they'd taken my recording studio, my gold records, and hundreds of hours of master tapes, there was no reason to despair.

They took my money, but they couldn't take my music.

So I vowed to tour harder and then started to retire my debt by releasing a double album called *The IRS Tapes*. (It's a winner, by the way. I recommend you buy a copy right away.)

I've heard people say I was singled out by the government because of my pot smoking or my politics, but the way I see it, there was a legitimate tax owed, it was the Feds' job to pursue it, and my job to pay it off.

There were a lot of numbers being tossed around in the press, but by the time the IRS had decided what I really owed, I'd paid much of it off. A settlement with the financial advisors who'd gotten me into the whole mess finished the trick, and finally my debt was paid.

And if I'd never been able to pay it off, I'd still be the same person I am today. I'd still love my family, I'd still have a lot of friends, and I'd still have my music.

It's easy to be overwhelmed by our desires for material things, but the fact is, most of us know what we truly value. Sometimes we just need a little reminder.

Of course, not everyone values the same things.

Not too long ago, my friend Ray Price called me up to tell me there was one thing he'd learned in life.

"What is it?" I asked.

And he said, "Money makes women horny."

The Willie Way 🖎

On the Road Again

If you're going to travel millions of miles and perform maybe ten thousand concerts in nearly every corner of the globe, it helps if it's in your nature to travel.

Even when I was a kid, I liked the idea of being on the road. My buddy Zeke and I used to hop freight trains to nowhere. And a lot of times, they actually stopped in the middle of nowhere and we'd have to turn around and make our way back home.

When there wasn't a train, Zeke and I would stick out our thumbs and hitch a ride. I generally didn't have any reason other than I wanted to see over yonder. I think Zeke just came along to see if anything interesting was going to happen. Today the section of road we used to hitchhike on between the towns of West and Hillsborough is called the Willie Nelson Highway. When Ann Richards was governor of Texas, she gave me a road sign with my name on it, and she didn't go through channels to have one made. Being a practical girl from just down the road in Waco, Ann sent a state trooper to Abbott with a set of tools and he just cut one down by the side of the road.

Good luck finding that road today, as the signs are taken down by fans as soon as they're put up. But if you want to drive the Willie Nelson Highway, it's right next to the railroad tracks in Abbott. The pavement's pretty much gone and it's just a gravel back road to nowhere. And that's the way I like it. Earlier this year, the state legislators were talking about naming a fancy new toll road for me. I said, "Thanks, but no thanks."

When you drive the Willie Nelson Highway, you drive free.

After I broke into the big time in the seventies, the band and I started selling out big arenas every night. For a while I liked to fly to these gigs and back home again in my private jet, but I got over that pretty quick. Maybe I missed the sound of the wheels on the highway.

My favored mode of transportation for most of my career has been my bus, the Honeysuckle Rose. I'm currently riding on Honeysuckle Rose number four, and it's a far cry from where we started. I've got a bedroom in the back—a king-size bed down at the floor level that has Indian jewelry and totems given to me by friends hanging all round it.

The Honeysuckle Rose, and a couple of great drivers— Gator and L.C.—have taken great care of me over the years. Not that we've been immune to problems.

We were driving down the highway in Canada a few years back when we had a terrible crash. What happened was that after getting in a fight with his wife, a guy pulled out on the highway with his lights off. He was bound to run into something, and unfortunately it turned out to be us doing sixty on our side of the road. I was on my bed in the back, Bobbie was in her bunk, Ben Dorsey and my son Billy were riding up front, and Gates was driving.

The other driver was in a little sports car, and he drove right into the front of the bus on the driver's side. If he'd been in a taller vehicle, Gates would never have walked again.

When we crashed, I sprung out of bed and kind of flew

into the middle of the bus. The motors were all dead and the lights and power were all off, and we were just flying down the highway. The steering was out, too, so Gates did the only thing he could; he just held on to the wheel trying to keep us upright. We raced along till the road got to a big curve and when we kept going straight, we were lucky that it was into a snowbank. Everyone on the bus walked away because Gator held on to that wheel.

Sometimes all you can do is hold on.

Roger Miller used to say, "He who lives by the song shall die by the road," but when that bus was going down, it occurred to me that I didn't intend to take him quite so literally.

Some musicians are happier in a plane, but I've noticed that when a plane plows into the turf, the chances of walking away aren't all that good.

So we got a new bus and went right back on the road. That's who we are.

Add it all up and I've spent more time on the road than off, and slept more nights on the bus than anywhere else. On the bus, I sleep like a baby. Sometimes I dream that I'm on the road, headed through the heart of America toward another town full of people who are coming to hear me sing. And when I wake up, I find that my dream has come true.

If you wonder what keeps me going back on the road again, the answer is obvious—I like to play music. The more I move around, the more people I get to play that music for.

Fame is a funny thing. For some people, the more famous they become, the more it seems to be a nuisance. Maybe it's because it took me so long to get where anyone knew my face, but I'm pretty comfortable with the idea of being recognized. If people don't know me, they're not going to come to the show.

A lot of people got to know me as the Red-Headed Stranger, but the fact is, I am never a stranger. The way I look at it, no matter where I'm at, I can walk outside and find somebody who knows me.

If I really need to talk to somebody, I can walk into any café or diner and always find someone who's happy to jaw a little. After my show, a lot of people I've met through the years drop by the bus to say hello. If they didn't drop by—or I didn't ever have time to see them—they wouldn't be old friends, they'd be former friends. Eventually we'd be strangers.

The bus gives me a place to meet and greet, and it also provides a place to hunker down and be alone. I'd just as soon have a plate of bacon and eggs on the bus at midnight than just about any meal in the fanciest restaurant in the world. That's just who I am. Still trying to get even with them pigs.

On the bus, we play chess and cribbage and keep up with the world by watching CNN and listening to a lot of great music. On the bus, I can also listen to whatever wants to speak to me. I guess I get my best reception on the bus.

I never forget that music has given me the freedom to move around, or that the bus is a good place to write. While I'm going down the highway, from somewhere in the great unknown, I hear a line or a melody, and the next thing I know, I've got a new song.

The road is filled with possibilities.

On the bus, jokes are a way of life, and I've found that the more good jokes you pass on, the more that are passed to you.

Next thing you know, people think you're a funny guy. And that reminds me . . .

A juggler is hurrying to his show when the cops pull him over for speeding.

"What are these matches and lighter fluid doing in your car?" the cop asks.

The juggler explains that he juggles torches in his act, and the cop says, "Oh, yeah? Let's see you do it."

So the juggler gets out and starts juggling the blazing torches.

While he's juggling fire, a couple driving by slows down and the husband says to his wife, "Wow! That drunk driving test is really getting tough!"

The bus takes me by a lot of fine golf courses, and by fine, I mean that they have something that looks like fairways, tees, and greens. The rest is just dressing.

I can stay out there on the road for a couple of months straight, but eventually the road tells me it's time to go home. And when that happens, we turn for Austin or Abbott or for an airport that can get me to Hawaii.

Roads are made by travel, not the other way around.

If we all ceased to travel, the roads would ultimately return to nature, though it might take a while, for we've built some very large roads.

I haven't been down all of them, but I'm working on it. Maybe I'm just waiting to see a guy at the side of the road juggling torches for a cop.

How High Is Up? ✎

Drive safe, drive sober—
the life you save may be my own.
　　—Willie's bumper sticker

Getting older has confirmed a whole lot of things that I instinctively knew all along. One is that honesty is always the best policy no matter the repercussions.

That's probably a big reason why just about every person who's ever heard my name or my music knows that I smoke pot. I know that displeases some people, but I still think that's better than making excuses about who I am and what I do.

So let's take a minute to talk about marijuana. If you're not interested in hearing what I have to say, no problem; there's a nice chapter on golf right after this one.

One place to start is in a typical American medicine or liquor cabinet. The highest killer on the planet is stress, and there aren't many people in America who don't medicate themselves one way or another.

Some people choose an occasional beer or a little pill the doctor prescribes, and I'm not knocking that. But the best medicine for stress is pot.

I think people forget that in all the "reefer madness" debate over marijuana, we're only talking about stems and seeds. That's all marijuana is, and I figure God must have made those stems and seeds for a reason.

As far as I can tell, the primary reasons and uses for the hemp plant are to smoke it, wear it, or use it to make fuel to burn in our cars. And I'm in favor of all three.

If you consider these views to be subversive to the general good, all I can say is that the truth is frequently subversive, but that doesn't mean it's not true.

No matter what I choose to do, I'm not trying to get anyone else to do anything he considers immoral or the law considers illegal. And that especially applies to America's kids. On the other hand, it seems pretty stupid to put people in jail because they have a small quantity of a plant that grows wild in large portions of the United States. And that especially applies to America's kids, far too many of whom are already in jail for nonviolent, pot-related offenses.

I don't know why pot agrees with me when alcohol and a lot of prescription drugs do not, but I suspect it has something to do with my Cherokee heritage. Among their many talents, the Cherokee were known and celebrated for carving ornate pipes. And I don't think they were carving those pipes just to look at.

According to Cherokee legend, in the beginning of man's days on earth, each tree, shrub, and herb agreed to furnish a remedy for one of the diseases of man. And each of these plants said they would appear to help man when he or she called upon them in their need.

In the world of the Cherokee, this was the origin of medicine.

The world of chemical pharmacology also traces its origins to the natural healing qualities of plants, every one of which has its use, if we only knew them as well as ancient man.

In addition to guidelines on the gathering and use of roots and herbs for healing, ancient Cherokee teachings also offered wisdom on reducing stress and finding harmony and balance in all our relationships. The general idea was that if you separated yourself from nature, you made yourself more prone to diseases, which were considered signs of being on the wrong path.

Of course we no longer live as the Cherokee lived, but I would no sooner wipe the hemp plant from the face of the earth than I would the rain forests of Brazil, which hold an untold and unchronicled treasure of healing plants.

The bottom line is that I'll support a war on drugs, but not a war on flowers and herbs. It's as simple as that—as simple as me asking what gives anyone the right to say that God was wrong to put them here.

If this conversation has stressed you out, I'd recommend a solution, but it might get me in trouble.

If you look at the results, it's pretty clear that the war on marijuana is a losing one. The latest dodge is to overrule state laws regarding marijuana use, growing, and possession—including the medicinal use of marijuana for terminal patients for whom no other drug will relieve their pain without drastic side effects.

No matter what you think about pot, it's up to the individual states to decide what to do about the single herb that best relieves the stress or the pain in the lives of people who need it.

Of course, that's just my opinion, and for all you know, I may be breaking the law as I write this.

As my doctor says, an ounce of prevention . . . costs a whole lot more than it used to.

Yesterday's Nine ⚡

When another is shooting, no player should talk, whistle,
hum, clink coins, or pass gas.
    —Willie's Rules of Golf

The only two good balls I hit at Willie's course
was when I stepped on the rake.
    —Kinky Friedman

Golf isn't just a game—it's an addiction.

Think of it as the crack cocaine of sports. Like most addictions, doing it more doesn't necessarily make you any better at it—it just makes you want more. Start with a few holes and the next thing you know, you've worked up to thirty-six a day. If the golf club manufacturers were smart, their advertising slogan would be, *"The first one's free."*

It's a difficult game to learn, and then it gets harder. I've been playing thirty-something years and have learned the hard way that just when you think you've figured it out, that's when you're really screwed.

My longest-running game has been at Pedernales Country Club, the nine-hole course I own in the hills outside of Austin. The course is a little rocky, but the greens roll true, and no one's ever going to tell you to tuck in your shirttail.

I first saw Pedernales playing in a celebrity tournament in the mid-seventies, and a couple of years later, another guy and I bought it. Then I let him have it, but later I bought it back. Then I lost it to the IRS, so Darrell Royal and Jim Bob Moffett bought it back for me. But the Feds said my pals didn't pay enough for it, so the IRS took it back and sold it to an Iranian fellow. We didn't get along, so I convinced a theater owner in Branson, Missouri, to buy it for me and I did six months of shows to pay him back. So I guess I've paid for the course several times.

For years, the standard game at Pedernales was somewhere between five and fifteen of us in an equal number of carts, all of us racing from shot to shot claiming whatever ball we found as our own.

The general philosophy in this game was, "May the man with the fastest cart win." Needless to say, I had a pretty fast cart.

If you're looking for gambling advice, I'd recommend playing for a foreign currency.

We used to play for a million pesos a hole, double on birdies. We didn't know what a million pesos were worth, but losing was considered catastrophic.

For big money or small, the rule from the first tee at Pedernales is "Hit till you're happy." If you don't use your mulligan on number one, you can't take it with you. The second hole is a par three, and I don't recommend playing a mulligan on a par three. You might hit it in the hole, and you don't want to waste the shot of a lifetime.

If you never have a bad lie, you never have to tell a bad lie.

If you're unhappy with your lie at Pedernales, you've got no one to blame but yourself. That's because we also have another local rule called the Pedernales Stroll, which lets you lift your ball from a rocky lie and stroll it someplace greener.

Ireland would be a little far, but otherwise I recommend that you drop the ball within one length of your arm.

Many years ago, some writer quoted me as saying, "Par at my course is whatever I say it is. Today I made a fourteen on the first hole and it turned out to be a birdie."

The only problem is, I don't remember saying it, and anyone who's played with me knows I'd pick up my ball long before making a fourteen. I'm not there to waste your time.

Pedernales has calmed down a bit in recent years, and I'd say I play more now for the love of the game than for the thrill of the party.

I must have been asked a thousand times what my handicap is. It's really high, but I can't tell you exactly because we might want to gamble some day. For starters, let's just say it's higher than yours.

Wives come and go, but a golf pro is forever.

Whether you own a golf course or just a golf habit, everyone needs a golf pro. Larry Trader has been my golf pro for more than half my life. I was playing honky-tonks in the sixties and having a little trouble collecting my money after the shows. There'd be five hundred people in the audience, but the owners would claim that maybe twelve of them had paid to get in. So Ray Price said he'd send a guy to help me out.

The next day, Trader drives up in a Cadillac convertible and gets out with a violin case under his arm. I'm not going to say what was in the case, but we never had any trouble collecting our money after that. The part about him being a golf pro was a side bet that I didn't know about.

———

For twenty years, Trader and I took on all comers in marathon matches for actual dollar amounts that my accountant requests I not mention. My game sucks, but when the shot is worth a thousand dollars, I tend to hit the ball a little better.

We once played a nine-hole match against Lee Trevino, the two of us picking our best shot against the Merry Mex playing solo. Lee shot a six under thirty on his own ball and we had to shoot twenty-nine to beat him. Way to go, Larry.

First, you've got to pick the right partner. Then make sure you win nine and eighteen.

People want to know everything about the golf swing, but Trader always told me to "just hit the ball." It's not anything special. Little kids usually hit it great the first swing. Lots of people do. But when they start getting instruction, they go all to hell. Kristofferson and I have been talking about making a golf instruction video. He has the worst swing in the world and I'm the worst teacher, so it's basically gonna be about cowboy-Zen golf. It's the only thing we know.

It's always better if you get a pro to tell you everything you're doing wrong. You can still keep doing it, but at least you'll know it's wrong.

One of my favorite rules on the scorecard at Pedernales is: "No bikinis, miniskirts, or skimpy see-through attire. Except on women."

A lot of musicians turn into golf fanatics, and that's because golf and music rely on tempo. Playing golf is a better high than most drugs, so some time in the eighties, the rock star's motto should have been changed to "sex, *golf*, and rock 'n' roll."

It's also easier to get a tee time for golf than it is for sex.

And that's okay with most golfers, because once in a blue moon all the different parts of the golf swing come together perfectly and you hit a golf shot that is so beautiful that it's *better* than an orgasm.

Tempo, a natural high, and deep, primal satisfaction—maybe sex, drugs, and rock 'n' roll have all been replaced by golf.

Golf is the last thing you should get mad about. The way I see it, if I play well, I'll have bested my opponent. If I want to play better, the way to do it is through positive thinking. Talk to yourself, be your own best friend; be the coach you always wanted in school.

If I continue to play bad, then what the hell—maybe I'll make my opponent feel better about *his* game. Either way, we'll be out under a beautiful sky, and my enjoyment of the hole, the game, and the day is not going to be dictated by something as haphazard as a golf swing.

Take my Hawaii golf buddy, Jim Fuller, for instance. Jim is the owner of Charlie's bar and restaurant, which is my favorite hangout on Maui. Jim and I have been playing golf for real money for going on thirty years. The first few years, I was giving him two strokes a hole, and I got so far ahead that I nearly won Charlie's from him. That made him get serious, so he took some lessons and now we play heads-up.

When I win a hole, I'm a hundred up on Maui, and that ain't bad. If I lose a hole, then I'm a hundred down, but I'm still on Maui, so what does it matter?

That doesn't mean we don't enjoy the competition. Last summer, I gave Jim a new big-headed driver and was up thousands of dollars while he tried to figure out how to hit it. But eventually he gave up on it and went back to hitting an iron off the tee, and we're running about even again.

A few years ago, I made a hole in one at the beautiful Dunes at Maui Lani Course. It wasn't a very long hole, and with the wind it took me a 2-iron to get there. Does that make me a short hitter or a really good golfer? Which would you choose?

With that in mind, I'll offer the two essential secrets of golf.

1. Don't lunge before you lurch.
2. The game of golf is not that different from the game of life.

Play to your strengths and try not to get too wrapped up in the outcome. Let things happen and someday you'll make a hole in one. I'm the living proof of that.

Like I always say, you can't lose 'em all.

> *Please leave the course*
> *in the condition you'd like to be found.*
> —Willie's Rules of Golf

Check Is Not the Same
as Mate 🪶

If you're not here, you're out of Luck.
    —sign at Luck, Texas, pop. 3

Luck, Texas is the centerpiece of what I call Willie World Headquarters—eight hundred acres of beautiful Texas comprised of golf course, recording studio, a cypress log cabin with a thirty-mile view of the Texas Hill Country, and my very own Western movie. We built the town for the filming of *Red-Headed Stranger*, and decided to name it Luck.

If you're not here, I always say, you're out of Luck.

When the bus pulls into Luck after a long stretch on the road, I can step outside to check on the dancing bay pony or my donkey—who's named Lucky, of course. I can also hop in the golf cart and drive across the road for a little golf.

Most of the time, I head up to Willie World Headquarters, the old saloon building where my friends drop by to play pool and chess, or tell me their latest crude joke, which might go something like this:

A ninety-year-old man goes to the doctor and says he wants to take Viagra. The doctor asks how much Viagra he thinks a man his age would need, and the old guy says, "Just enough so I don't piss on my shoes."

As you might guess by that joke, there's nothing fancy about Luck. We do have hot and cold running water, but you have to be patient, because the hot water is generally in the summer and the cold in the winter, which is okay because it helps prevent the possibility of a shock to your system.

Occasionally we play a little music at the headquarters. The back room has a little piano and a Macintosh audio system. With the brilliant help of producer Joe Gracey, I've recorded several great albums there, including one of my favorites, *The Rainbow Connection,* with my daughters Paula and Amy.

When we record at the headquarters, I use the best pickers around. You can drive all over town and you won't find any better musicians, and it won't take you more than a minute to do it.

We also like to play a little chess.

Not too long ago when Turk and I hatched the idea of this little book, we decided we'd sit down at Luck and discuss a few of the things we did and didn't know over a game of chess.

Though I'm no longer what you'd consider a drinking man, and I frown at the flaunting of federal laws regarding the brewing of illegal beverages, I felt that Turk needed a little moonshine to help him concentrate on the game. Not wanting him to drink alone, of course, I drew two small glasses of clear liquid from a wooden cask on the bar.

Between sips of moonshine and coffee, the game and the conversation began when I moved out my first pawn and said, "Checkmate."

With a confused look on his face, Turk said, "Play you again for a hundred."

Making his first move, Turk started with what he's learned in fifty years of tallness. "Every sucker thinks he's a wise guy," he told me.

"Travel light," I countered. "Carry a small suitcase and a smaller ego."

"It doesn't matter how heavy something is," he told me as he rudely took my pawn. "What matters is how long you have to hold it."

"Good golfers don't listen to bad caddies," I lied.

"Bad caddies don't listen to anyone," Turk replied. At least I think that's what he said, as he was also gagging on moonshine at the moment.

"Okay," I said. "Good bartenders don't listen to bad drunks."

"The last drink," he said as he took my knight, "is always a mistake."

He had me three pieces down at this point and was clearly falling into my trap, though I wasn't quite sure yet what the trap was.

"Safe sex is better than lite beer," I told him.

"The devil doesn't drink lite beer," he said.

"And God doesn't drink decaf," I replied.

"Honesty may be the best policy," he reminded me, "but it may not be the cheapest."

"Horseshit," I told him. And to tell you the truth, he looked a little hurt. "Horseshit," I explained. "All the whipped cream in the world won't improve it."

Realizing I'd also taken his bishop, he didn't reply, so I added one more thought to his confusion.

"Breast-feeding."

"What about it?"

"Nothing. Just breast-feeding."

We thought about that awhile, then got back to the wisdom at hand.

"Listening is more mysterious than talking," he told me.

At least I think that's what he said. I wasn't really paying attention.

I'm not exactly sure who said what after that, but I believe it went something like this.

"Work for yourself."

"The best bets in Vegas are casino stocks."

"Beautiful women are trouble."

"All women are beautiful."

By this time, check was flying back and forth and pieces were sailing off the board like chickens in a tornado. The only real question was whether we were going to run out of pieces of wisdom before we ran out of chess pieces. Either way, it was only a matter of time. All kings must fall.

"No one story is true," Turk told me. "They all are."

"Did you write that?" I asked in awe.

"No," he confessed. "Hemingway. And Shakespeare wrote the Bible.

"So give it your best shot," Turk said. "What's the best advice?"

"The early bird may get the worm, but the second mouse gets the cheese."

"What does the first mouse get?" he asked.

"You'll find out soon enough," I warned as I slid my rook down opposite his king.

"Checkmate," I said. "This time for real."

"Dang," he replied.

"Breakfast of astronauts," I replied. "How about another game?"

"Why not?"

Then pulling out his wallet, Turk laid a hundred-peso note on the table and said, "Double or nothing."

Obviously he's known me too long.

A Healing State 🖎

I am a cowboy
I am a sailor
I have drifted far and wide
I have crossed the seven oceans
I have crossed the Great Divide.

But if you're ever looking for me
Let me tell you where I'll be.
I'll be somewhere soaking up sunshine
On my island in the sea.
    —Willie Nelson, "Island in the Sea"

Since the first time I visited Maui, I've felt that I had a relationship with the island and its people. The first time I went there, I liked the place so much, I bought a house.

I didn't know much about Hawaiian cowboys until I got there, but I learned pretty fast and quickly made some lifelong friends. The Paniolos can handle horses and cows as well as any man or woman on earth, and relax by playing traditional Paniolo music on the Hawaiian slack key guitar.

When you go up-country, which is just about anywhere away from the beach and farther up the volcano, it's amazing how much the land is like Texas. I've always said there's not that much difference between sailors and cowboys anyway.

———

Hawaii has been very good to me. Last year I rode horseback into the Haleakala crater at the top of the island of Maui. I was riding with the forest ranger who services the hike-in cabins there, and the first day we were seven hours in the saddle riding across a landscape like the moon. Sore butt, hottest I've ever been in the day, freezing cold at night—and we just kept saying, "Wow, what a good time!"

Like Austin, Maui has a healthy music scene and a strong sense of community. I'll never give up Texas, but Annie, the boys, and I have pretty much made Maui our home. Where else can I follow an early morning run on the beach with a breakfast among friends at Charlie's? A quick round of golf at the nine-hole Maui Country Club might be followed by chess in my backyard club-house, Django's Orchid Lounge, where the smell of blooming orchids mixes with the fresh salt air to remind me that I'm in paradise.

The fogs and dense forests of the Iao Valley are my favorite part of the whole island, maybe the whole world, but Maui seems good wherever I go.

A lot of people say the winding road to Hana is the most beautiful drive on earth, and I'm not likely to argue with them. The Hana Highway also leads me to the home of my fellow Highwayman, Kris Kristofferson. Kris and I have made five or six movies together, and played a whole lot of music and golf, and I'd walk across hot lava for the guy.

Maybe it's because he lives in Hana, but Kris never needs a thing from me, which makes us the best kind of friends, ones who are always glad to see each other.

Woody Harrelson also makes his home in Hana, and Woody is a friend I depend upon to keep me up-to-date on living a life that is respectful of the world around us.

Of all the places I've been on earth, Maui is the most spiritual. The ancient cultures that populated Maui and the other Hawaiian islands clearly recognized this as a special place—a place where man and nature could live together in harmony.

There's a good deal of evidence that the Hawaiian people came here from Polynesia, which meant they either were really lost or had an impressive knowledge of sailing and navigation.

There are other interesting theories about the origins of human-kind on Hawaii. One of my favorites relates to the end of the early civilization we know as Atlantis. Knowing that their great city was going to sink, the Atlantians are said to have built great ships and sailed west, circled what is now South America, and then separated, with each ship charting its own destiny.

There's no proof that this happened, as this would have been many thousands of years before Christ walked on the earth, but the theory is that the warriors of Atlantis went to Samoa (where their descendants include some really big dudes). The fishermen of Atlantis sailed to the Aleutian Islands, Alaska, and the Northwest— one of the richest fisheries on earth. And finally there were the navigators and doctors, who came to Hawaii and founded a culture that has lasted thousands of years.

So did this really happen? Who knows? I like it because it explains so much about parallels in language, culture, architecture, and religious beliefs that exist in places that modern science tells us had no communication until relatively modern times. Mysteries do not need to be dissected and proven to have meaning to us. Meaning is where we find it, and what we make of it.

What I have made from my connections to Hawaii and its stories is a deeper appreciation for the island's ancient mysteries and how they can help me understand who we are and where we came from.

Another of my friends on the island, Kimo Alo, is a Kahuna

priest and traditional Hawaiian healer. Modern medicine is just beginning to understand the value and methods of traditional herbalists and ancient healing traditions, and all I can say is that the Kahunas did wonders for me.

Plagued by a bad back and my system poisoned from years of drinking too much alcohol and eating bad food, twenty years ago I accompanied Kimo to a secret place in the mist-shrouded heights of Maui and underwent a healing regimen based on plants and massage that most Western doctors would have discounted completely.

But within days I felt better than I had in many years, and was soon able to ride bareback across the slopes of the volcano with the sweet Hawaiian winds fresh in my face and my braids flying along behind me.

Thank you, Kimo.

But the most lasting influence I've had from my contacts with the Kahunas has been even greater than the healing of my ailing back. Kimo tells me that it is impossible to harness our own physical powers unless we first learn of the greater power of love.

I find it curious that wherever you go on earth, the fundamental teachings remain the same. Underlying everything is the simple idea of love.

The Willie Way 🕊

Physical and Spiritual

On or off the road, I've got to exercise just about every day. If I didn't work to keep in good shape, I couldn't tour the way I do, or sing nearly as long every night.

In high school, I played football, basketball, baseball, and ran track. And one thing I can tell you, when Jesus said "Love thy neighbor," there was no such thing as high school football.

When you get older, you've got to find a way to replace all the sports you can't do anymore. On the road, I play golf or I jog. More than once, I've gone jogging in a town I don't know and had to knock on a stranger's door and ask directions to get back to where I started.

I still box a bit, too. I've got a speed bag hanging in the bedroom of the bus, and I can put on some gloves and work out on it when we've got a long drive. Trying to throw a roundhouse when Gator is changing lanes on the highway either keeps me on my toes or dumps me on my ass.

I feel a lot healthier now than I did thirty years ago, and that tells me that thirty years ago, I was pretty messed up.

I've seen a lot of guys hit their seventies and decide they ought to just sit down for a while. The problem is, the longer you sit, the harder it is to get back up again. It used to upset me when I'd meet a fat doctor with a drink in one hand and a cigarette in the other who told me I should give up pot or that running wasn't good for a guy my age. There are some good doctors out there, but if they tell you not to exercise, the first thing I'd do is change doctors.

My stretching routine is part of what keeps me going. I'm not sure you have to stretch in any exact way, but it helps to get some knowledgeable instruction. My routine is part yoga, part Hawaiian Kahuna medicine, and part oriental martial arts. I'm particularly fond of standing on my head while the bus is rolling down the highway. What a rush.

I've been interested in martial arts most of my life. When I was a kid, I read about these strange Oriental arts like jujitsu and judo, and how a little guy, with the right body twist, could throw a big guy.

Well, I was a little guy, so this was stuff I just had to learn!

When I got to Nashville, I studied kung fu, expecting to learn to protect myself better and be tougher when I got in a scrape. When you're singing in a roadhouse full of drunk cowboys and one of them thinks you've been making eyes at his girlfriend, it's good to be able to defend your territory. But the main thing I learned from kung fu was the simple power of patience.

The discipline that's done the most for me is Tae Kwon Do. A decade ago, my boys started taking Tae Kwon Do; then my wife got into it, too. Well, the boys keep getting bigger every year, and Annie's getting tougher, so you can see the problem I was faced with. It didn't take me long to realize that I'd better start studying with their teacher in Austin, Master Um.

Tae Kwon Do is a Korean martial art that began as a form of unarmed self-defense, and which helps you achieve greater physical, mental, and artistic skills. The overall goal is to improve your level of fitness, confidence, self-discipline, and concentration.

It takes all of those to learn that flying side kick, which is the symbol of Tae Kwon Do. I was sixty-nine years old when I earned my black belt, and the hardest part was a spinning back kick to break two boards. Even if my body's not a blur as it whirls around, my long braids fly pretty fast, so maybe I could break a board or two with those.

Johnny Cash was still with us at the time, and when I told him about my black belt, Johnny said, "Oh, that ain't nothing—I know a seventy-four-year-old woman with a black belt."

But that didn't faze me. I just said, "Bring her on!"

To All the Girls I've Loved 🖎

Summer sun, no prettier than summer rain
Summer gone, summer coming back again
Another love, lost in the great divide.
   —Willie Nelson, "The Great Divide"

Did you hear the story about the couple that's been married sixty years? They come downstairs for breakfast on their sixtieth anniversary, and the husband says, "Do you remember sixty years ago, the morning after we were wed, when we both sat naked at breakfast?"

And his wife says, "We're not so old; we could do that again."

So they take off all their clothes and sit down to breakfast, and the wife says, "Not that much has changed; you still make my nipples hot."

And her husband says, "I'm not surprised—one's in your coffee and the other's in your oatmeal!"

If you're married and don't find that one to be funny, wait twenty or thirty years and the joke will be on you. And I sincerely hope your marriage does last another twenty or thirty because the only thing worse than being married is being single.

One of the greatest sources of happiness in life is through your appreciation of the opposite sex. And if it's not the opposite sex that turns you on, I suggest you go to iTunes and download my cut of Ned Sublette's fine song "Cowboys Are Frequently Secretly Fond of Each Other."

For me, though, it's about the ladies.

My appreciation of women first blossomed with Mama Nelson, who started me on the road to life and was still there for me when I took the road out of town.

And though my mother, Myrtle, wasn't there very much when I was young, I later came to appreciate her own loving ways, and always enjoyed taking my fellow musicians like Ray Price and Kris Kristofferson to Myrtle and her husband Ken's home in the Northwest. Didn't matter when we showed up, she always fed us and blessed us and sent us on our way. And God bless her for that.

I have noticed that for some reason, women have always loved me.

I've done my best to love them in return, and generally got along well with them—until we got married, that is. Now on marriage number four, I think I've about got it figured out, but it did take me a while.

Four marriages might lead you to believe that I'm a quitter, but consider this: those four marriages have lasted a total of fifty years, which is over ninety percent of my adult life, so I guess I'm better at being married than I am at being single.

My first marriage, to Martha, who was tempered like hot iron, was a roller-coaster ride from the beginning till the end, and we did more than our share of fighting. Instead of fighting we should have been talking, but we were facing the number one problem in most marriages.

Too many married people don't know how to listen to each other.

You hear women say their man doesn't listen to them, but the truth is neither of the sexes is worth a damn at listening to each other. And that's the beginning of the end, because once you get the feeling that your husband or your wife doesn't listen to what you say, then your chances of opening up and saying what you truly feel are slim and none.

When you start talking to yourself instead of to your spouse, it's only a matter of time till the proverbial shit hits the fan.

Ladies, if you want your husband to listen to you, don't forget to offer him some encouragement in the midst of your tales of woe.

Encouragement from a woman is the most inspiring thing a man can hear.

Guys, if you want your wife to hear you, offer her some support. If you don't support her now with word and deed, chances are you'll be supporting her later with your paycheck. I didn't listen well for way too long and the result was that I ended up buying quite a few houses that I didn't end up living in. Despite that, I don't regret buying a single one of them.

One thing I've learned is that there is no such thing as an ex-wife.

If you had a relationship, just because you don't live with that person anymore doesn't mean they're a non-human being. If someone's been a part of your life, that part of your life can be neither erased nor forgotten.

If the whole marriage thing doesn't work out, you can always try to live monogamously. Good luck with that. One thing I've noticed is we are not made to be alone.

Did you hear about the man and woman astronaut who go to Mars?

Turns out there's Martians everywhere and they look quite a bit like humans. So the astronauts decide that they should each have sex with a Martian—purely in the interest of science, of course.

While the man astronaut goes to a bar to buy a Martian chick some drinks, the woman astronaut grabs a Martian man and says, "Let's do it."

They go back to the spaceship, the Martian man takes off his clothes, and she's pretty disappointed at what she sees.

"You want bigger?" asks the Martian man. Then he twists his right ear and is suddenly very long!

The Earth woman still looks disappointed, so the Martian man twists his left ear and adds a bit of girth to match.

So the two of them go at it all night long. The next morning the woman astronaut asks the male astronaut how it went with his Martian chick.

And he says, "Great, but she almost twisted my ears off!"

The most recent wedding in my clan was my daughter Paula's. Paula is one of the sweetest girls who ever lived, and I was playing golf at Pedernales a few hours before the wedding when she came running across the fairway, threw her arms around me, and hugged me close. You don't have to be a psychologist to know how happy that made me.

In a couple of hours, Paula would be marrying a guy she really loved, and she was just as excited as she deserved to be. We talked a bit about the ceremony and all the family that was already on their way to the wedding, and when she bounced back to the house, I could see her happiness in every step she took.

After she was gone, I stood there trying to remember if I'd ever been that happy. I thought back to my childhood, a time and a place where young people generally got married because they had to.

When I was a young man in Abbott, we could sleep with anybody that would have us, but if you got a girl pregnant, you had to marry her.

Factually speaking, it's not premarital sex until you actually get married.

Not only was our approach to sex a lot of fun, but I've noticed lately as I spend time in Abbott that a lot of those marriages ended up lasting a very long time. So what exactly was it that those teenagers were doing wrong?

Paula's wedding was just beautiful, and I got so filled up with appreciation for my life and my family that I nearly exploded like the Fourth of July. Paula is named for her godfather, Paul English, my drummer and best friend of forty years. And when the minister asked, "Who gives this bride?" I cracked everybody up by saying, "Me and Paul."

That of course is the name of one of my best songs, which celebrates the forty-plus years Paul and I have been together on the road. Come to think of it, counting Paul, I've probably been married five times. Like I said, cowboys are frequently secretly fond of each other.

When my third marriage, to Connie, fell apart, I never dreamed I'd get married again. I already had a great bunch of kids—Lana, Susie, Billy, Paula, and Amy—and figured I'd reached my quota on love.

But I had forgotten one important thing—there is no limit on love.

Luckily, you don't have to know of your own potential for something great to come of it. After three marriages, I certainly didn't dream that I would marry so well or that I'd have two more fine boys. Between Annie and my boys Lukas and Micah, and all my early family, I feel like the luckiest son of a gun in the whole wide world.

Some people say we make our own luck, but that would practically make me a luck factory.

———

It's easier now to be on the road and be married. That's partially because Annie is as independent as I am. We've done our best to allow each other to be ourselves. She tolerates me being on the road; I like having a home to go home to. That's pretty hard to beat.

So Annie and the boys hold down the home front in Hawaii, and they also come out on the road with me during the summer tour. Both of the boys play in my band—Micah on drums, Lukas on lead guitar—and I think there's a lot of great music in their futures.

I guess the main thing that's different about my approach to marriage now is that I finally started to let things happen. Instead of trying to make everything happen, I just get out of the way and let it happen. That's one of the biggest things I've learned, and once I did it, my relationships with everybody improved.

After fifty years of marriage, I guess I realized I'm just the marrying type.

Do the Right Thing 🌱

Biodiesel

Higher Good is like water,
it benefits us all.
　　　—The *Tao Te Ching*

As soon as you admit to yourself that everything good you do comes back to you twenty times over, then your life will change in incredible ways. Doing things because they're the right thing to do—not just because of some tangible gain you've planned—will ultimately reward you in better ways than money, power, comfort, or fame.

You may have never heard of biodiesel fuels, but I believe strongly that biodiesel is something that can benefit all of us in a great number of ways.

Biofuels are motor fuels that are made from farm products. They can be made from crops grown specifically to make fuel, from crop by-products, or just from recycled products such as used French fry oil. The world fries a lot of potatoes and all that recycled vegetable oil can be put to use to power millions of vehicles.

My wife and I both started driving environmentally friendly cars that basically run on vegetable oil. Let me tell you, the first time I pulled up to Pacific Biodiesel to fill up my new Mercedes (which runs on regular diesel), the Mercedes people were really worried about it. But the car ran perfectly, and the more I drove it, the more I got interested in the biodiesel business so I could convince others to join us.

Next thing I knew, I was a partner in a company that produces a new fuel called Bio-Willie. Of course, if you've got a fuel to sell, you need a place to sell it, so I also began to make deals with truck stops all over Texas to sell it.

As fate would have it, around the same time I started a biodiesel business, I also won my favorite truck stop, Carl's Corner, in a poker game. My first reaction to this stroke of luck was that I ought to lose it back as soon as possible, because Carl didn't seem all that sad to see it go.

Since Carl built the place and the town that surrounds it on I-35 south of Hillsboro—and also knows everything about running it—the two of us are partners now. We've made a few upgrades and have built a music theater atop the old swimming pool, hot tub, and striptease stage. Unlike a lot of truck stops, we serve healthy food, not a plateful of grease; we've got great coffee, not a pot of burnt grounds; and we have great Texas bands and songwriters, and live gospel music on Sundays.

But the most important thing we do is sell biodiesel. By the time you read this, we think biodiesel will be available in almost every part of America. That setup will allow me fill up my car or my bus with biodiesel when on the road—and will do the same for a high percentage of all Americans. In the meantime, I've got a 700-gallon tank on the hill in Austin that lets me fill up there.

And instead of smelling like burnt diesel, my exhaust smells like French fries, popcorn, and doughnuts, which causes women on diets to follow me everywhere I go.

One evening I fell asleep in the garage with the engine running, and when I woke up, I'd gained five pounds!

Ha! Just checking to see if you can tell a joke from the facts.

The reasons to use biofuels in this country are numerous. For starters, they burn cleaner than traditional fossil fuels and that makes them better for the environment and better for the air we breathe. Biodiesel reduces carbon dioxide emissions up to eighty percent, particulate emissions up to seventy-five percent, and sulfur emissions up to a hundred percent. One of my bus drivers, Tony Sizemore, has allergies that are aggravated by regular diesel fumes, and now that his bus runs on biodiesel, he can stand by the generator exhaust and not even notice it's on. (Tony, by the way, has been driving the same Florida coach bus for me for twenty years, and recently set an amazing record as the first driver in one bus on one tour to log a million miles! Congratulations, big guy, we've made it to the moon and back twice together.)

Compared to traditional diesel fuels, biodiesel is also safer to handle, helps diesel engines run quieter and last longer, and—just in case there's a spill—breaks down in the environment much faster.

More important, biofuels can start us back on the overdue road to energy independence. As I write this, in America we think gas at two or two and a half dollars a gallon is outrageously expensive. But in Europe, they're already paying three or four times that much, and I don't know anyone who expects fuel prices to go anywhere but up.

Whatever your opinion about the war in Iraq, you can't ignore the fact that we spent hundreds of billions of dollars fighting a war in a place that has a lot of energy resources. The end result of that war won't be known for a long time, but there is really no need going around starting wars over oil when we have what we need right here at home. And no, we don't have to start eating French fries three meals a day, because farmers can grow crops that are planted and harvested just to fuel our cars.

With the help of a lot of other dedicated musicians, I've spent twenty years raising money and awareness about the plight of

America's family farmers. For twenty years I've been telling any-body who'd listen that we haven't been taking care of our small farmers or our small businesses. We've been allowing big corpora-tions to come in and take over the land, and that is a huge mistake. At one point, America had eight million small family farmers. Now we have fewer than two million, and are still losing three to five hundred a week.

Corporate farming operations have taken over some of the land that those farmers have been forced to leave, but much of it re-mains fallow and abandoned. Put it all together, and you have a country with a million acres of unused farmland, a million out-of-work farmers, and a desperate need for alternative fuels.

Here's an idea: when you can grow your own motor fuel, everyone will want to be a farmer or own part of a farming business.

Because of growing demand for biofuels, there's going to be a strong incentive to see more small farmers back on the land. If we truly want to make our country energy-independent, we need a biofuel homestead act to put America's farmers back to work on that land, growing sunflowers and other crops to make our vehi-cles go.

Putting families back on the land would revitalize small towns and cities all across America and reverse a fifty-year decline in Middle America.

Because the efforts of these families would be for the common good, we should be able to set a price that guarantees they don't lose money. If they work five hundred acres of fallow land for five years, then the land would be theirs to operate and to pay taxes on, taxes that will support local services and schools.

———

If you're wondering who's going to burn all this biodiesel, there are already a lot of diesel vehicles in this country, and most of them can run biodiesel as well as or better than the fuel they've been buying.

The very first diesel engine was designed to run on peanut oil, and the fact that most people don't know that shows just how hard the oil companies have worked to maintain their monopoly on motor fuels. But oil companies now know we're running out of oil and they want in on the growing market for alternate fuels. I don't want to exclude the big boys from this vast new energy market, because the big oil companies are just the partners we need to help get this done on a big scale.

Right off the bat, we have tens of thousands of school buses that run on diesel, and those engines wouldn't have to be converted in any way for them to run on biofuels. Within a year, we could have millions of kids headed to school in buses that pollute less and make all of us think of French fries when they drive by. That alone ought to be enough to get McDonald's to back us.

When you add it up, biodiesel costs no more than fossil-fuel diesel, runs just as good, and puts Americans to work rather than sending our money to the Middle East and other parts of the world.

We all know it's time for America to once again be a leader in world energy production. It's also time for America as a country to stand up and proclaim loudly that we believe in a cleaner environment.

To make that happen, we need Congress, farmers, and consumers to work together.

The single best reason to make this happen is that it's the right thing to do. The first few years, you may have to actually plan where you're going to fuel up with biodiesel, but choosing to do it anyway because it's the right thing to do is going to be a powerful positive force in your life. Every minute you drive that car, you're going to know you're doing the right thing and you'll be driving down the street with a smile on your face.

We're all going to the same place, my friends—a place called the future—and we're all going to get there at the same time. Only some of us are going to get there by having had a smile on our faces for much of our lives.

Choose to do the right thing in your life, and you're choosing to empower yourself and the country you love. It seems so simple.

Fool on the Hill 🖋

There's an old saying in Tennessee—I know . . . it's in Texas,
probably in Tennessee—that says, fool me once, shame on—
shame on you. Fool me—you can't get fooled again.
  —George W. Bush

All men are fools, but only wise men know it.
  —The *Tao Te Ching*

My golf course, recording studios, and Luck, Texas, Western Town
are all three located atop tall hills. I don't know if that makes me
the fool on the hill, but the idea has its appeal.

The idea of the fool on the hill predates the Beatles by a few
thousand years. Even the Tao is said to have originated with her-
mits who seem to have been like the proverbial wise man on the
mountaintop. You'd have to be one part fool to choose life in a
damp cave.

Both the fool and the wise man know that on the mountaintop
you don't have to be anything but yourself. On the mountaintop, you can burp and fart without saying "excuse me."

And if you manage to burp and fart at the same time, you may
realize that you are a true master.

On the mountaintop—as you can in the forest, floating down a
river, or sitting by the shore—you can learn about yourself by listening to the rhythms and melodies of nature surrounding you.

If I'd been a Zen master in ancient times or a clown in the

king's court, I'd probably have told everyone to simply shut up and listen for a change.

When it comes to the national debate on the status of Social Security, a wise man might say, "If it ain't broke, don't fix it."

On the other hand, a fool might say, "If it ain't broke, break it."

No amount of brains can prevent you from playing the fool for love—been there, done that—and we've had more than our share of fools on Capitol Hill. But unlike the kings of old, today's leaders are probably too thin-skinned to tolerate a cabinet jester occasionally knocking the stuffing out of their ego when they get to feeling too high and mighty.

Dang, where's Will Rogers when we need him?

There's a big difference between being an idjit and a fool, between the devil and his ignorance and one of God's holy clowns. And the difference is both in the heart and in the mind.

A lot of my best friends have been clowns. They didn't all wear red noses like Turk did when he was the opening act for some of my shows in his MUCH younger days, or dive into a barrel just before an angry bull sent it flying like the fearless Leon Coffee.

Perhaps I'm drawn to foolishness, but I've had plenty of other pals who seemed to stumble through life in one extended pratfall. And the lack of clown shoes didn't reduce their ability to find a joke whenever one was needed.

Asleep at the Wheel's Ray Benson wears a size 17, which means he's in clown shoes all day long, even when he plays golf. The last time we teed it up, Ray had this piece of wisdom for me.

What do you call a beautiful woman on a caddie's arm?

A tattoo.

———

Roger Miller, who may have been the king of clowns, said his pappy was a pistol, which made him a son of a gun. Only a clown searching for a rhyme for the word purple would come up with "maple surple."

When a cop pulled Roger over for erratic driving and said, "Can I see your license?" Roger replied, "Can I shoot your gun?"

Roger was practically the patron saint of holy fools. A holy fool sees the world in his own unique way and sticks with it. For Roger, there was no cow too sacred to roast, no chicken too sacred to pluck.

By other people's standards, that may seem like a dumb way to do things, but for the fool, it works. From the fool's perspective, the rest of us are the fools. And so it falls to fools to point out our weaknesses. And it rises to them to act, not as society commands, but according to their own understanding of what is right and wrong.

The holy fool's version of the Golden Rule would be, "Undo the others, and maybe they'll undo you right back again."

The point—other than a good laugh, which is point enough— is that a sense of humor will often get you through hard times better than good times will get you through no sense of humor.

Take the IRS, for instance (and I wish you would). When I suddenly found myself in debt up to my ears to the Feds, a sense of humor about what seemed like a hopeless situation helped me hold on to my sense of self.

Maybe I was a fool not to have worried more about the situation at the time, but worry didn't seem as practical as hard work. After my debt was paid, all I'd lost were things I didn't need anyway.

When the weather's nice in Texas—which means just about anything short of a tornado—I like to sleep out by a nice fire at my campground on a meadow near the top of the hill at Luck.

A group of us sit around picking guitars, looking at stars, and passing the bullshit around till we get sleepy.

Maybe it's just the height of the hill, but when I'm there, I feel closer to God. Being close to God doesn't mean he's going to speak to me (and if he speaks to you, I'd like to try some of what you're smoking).

There are infinite ways to be close to God. You can dance in the light—or in the firelight, whirl like a dervish, float in the ocean, or sing like a Baptist choir. Speaking of which . . .

Why don't Baptists make love standing up?
They're afraid someone will think they're dancing.

When a fool climbs a hill to be close to God, the real reason is that the fool is trying to distance himself from the things and ways that are far from God.

Teddy Roosevelt advised us, "Keep your eyes on the stars and your feet on the ground." A fool might need a hill to accomplish that, but a true sage can do it anywhere.

America the Beautiful ✍

If America could sing with one voice,
it would be Willie's.
　　　　—Emmylou Harris

After thousands of shows spanning sixty years, it would be impossible to pick just one gig as my all-time favorite. My sixtieth birthday concert at Austin City Limits was pretty great, but so were all the Farm Aid concerts. The Greek Theater in L.A. was fun in 2004. Red Rocks in Colorado is spectacular every year, and it's always good to get back to Austin for my annual shows at Stubb's Bar-b-q and The Backyard.

Like I said—impossible to choose a favorite.

And it's just as hard to pick a favorite song from a particular show. Most nights I play fifty or sixty songs and I like them all or I wouldn't sing them.

But there is one recent memory—one song, one emotional moment—that's stayed with me pretty well.

Like most Americans, I was pretty torn up in the period following 9/11. So when the producers of the 9/11 memorial concert *A Tribute to Heroes* called to ask me to sing "America the Beautiful" on the national television broadcast, I was glad to be invited to sing a beautiful song for my country.

At the time I agreed to do it, I had no idea where I was going to be in the bill, and as it turned out, I was scheduled to sing at the end of the show. That felt like quite an honor, but on the other hand, as I watched the other artists perform, I was really getting emotional. The whole show was spontaneous and genuine, so by the time I got around to doing my part, I was already very moved.

Sometimes when you sing, you can feel the audience right there with you, and singing "America the Beautiful" that evening, I felt as if I was with all of America, and all of America was there with me.

The spirit of American unity that I felt that evening—and throughout the period following 9/11—is a spirit that we should all try to hold on to. I'd like to see us build upon what started then, and work toward a raising of the spirit and a period of good positive thinking.

To do that, we don't have to share the same political opinions any more than we have to like the same music. We just have to remember that America has always been a diverse group of people who share a belief in freedom and democracy.

When you consider the importance of those ideas, it's sometimes difficult to understand why we spend so much time arguing amongst ourselves.

When we listen to the words of "America the Beautiful"— written by Katharine Lee Bates in 1893—the things that unite us are so much easier to see.

"Crown thy good with brotherhood, from sea to shining sea."

One thing that could bring us all closer together here at home is to remember that our sense of brother- and sisterhood shouldn't stop at the borders of our nation. Just because we were lucky enough to be born here—or welcomed here from some other place— doesn't mean that any one of us is more important than any one else on this planet. The love that we feel for our nation doesn't diminish the love we feel for our families. The same thing can be said for the love we feel for our fellow men and women all over the world.

It's a little sad that it takes a disaster like 9/11 or the tsunami to bring us together, but together is where we belong—in good times and in bad. And the more we show the rest of the world that we care about them, the better it will be for all of us.

For more than two hundred years, this nation has stood tall and shone brightly as the lighthouse of freedom to the entire world.

"Crown thy good with brotherhood."

And it's all right there in the song.

Willie Nelson for President! ⤸

Sageliness within and kingliness without.
　—The *Tao Te Ching*

I don't make jokes.
I just watch the government
and report the facts.
　—Will Rogers

Don't panic! Even though this chapter is called "Willie Nelson for President," let's get one thing straight. I do NOT want to make a run for the Oval Office.

There are far too many roaches in my closet for me to go into politics.

I have known a lot of presidents and am close to Jimmy Carter, who brought a clear mind and a good heart to Washington, and did what he thought was best for this country, without regard to how those actions would affect his popularity.

In most recent administrations, it seems like the actions of the president are too often based on appealing to some base or special interest group, or merely on getting reelected, and I think America has suffered because of it.

Maybe Carter had the right idea after all. And maybe Clinton *should* have inhaled.

———

Jimmy's son, Chip Carter, and I have talked about the possibility of my being his running mate in a presidential race. Chip wants to eliminate taxes on everyone who makes less than $30,000 a year.

My platform is that after we're elected, everyone has to get a gonorrhea shot.

Even though I'll never be president, I do have some ideas about the responsibilities of the office.

In the way of the Tao, a good ruler is one who allows and encourages the people to fulfill their work and to pursue the endeavors of their choice.

This country is blessed to have the greatest founding documents of any nation in history. There are always a bunch of politicians who want to pass amendments to our constitution, but their position generally reveals their own blind eye to the simple fact that the Constitution and the Bill of Rights are there to guarantee our freedoms, not to restrict them.

If you're going to be an elected official, it's important to remember that you were elected to serve the people, not yourself, your friends, and your business interests.

For fifty years, this nation's lawmakers have passed farm legislation that favors big business over families. And I don't just mean over farm families, because every family in America has the right to a safe, healthy food supply, clean air, clean water, and a healthy environment. To compromise any of those by claiming we're trying to protect American jobs is a sham on the American people.

Millions of farmers is what I call more jobs than a few hundred thousand farmers. Generating electricity at home through renewable resources like biofuels, wind power, and solar and geothermal sources would create countless jobs for Americans, while importing energy only sends our dollars—and our young men and women in the military—overseas. Many of those dollars—and far too many of those young people—never come home again.

Preserving and protecting our natural resources and expanding our national parks would generate more American jobs, and bring untold numbers of tourists from overseas who could help reverse the growing trade imbalance.

This is not rocket science, but taking the money we're about to waste on a trip to Mars and dedicating it to science education for all young Americans would create a new generation of American scientists who would once again put us at the forefront of technology and innovation.

Damn, this sounds so good, maybe I *should* run.

But like a lot of people who are much more qualified than me, I'd be crazy to spend years of my life and millions of dollars trying to get the most votes as a presidential candidate.

The reason is that the candidate with the most votes does not always win the presidency. Ask Al Gore, who received two million more votes than George W. Bush. How does that work—to win big and lose bigger?

So let's talk some good old-fashioned common sense about why the founding fathers' faith in the electoral college is no longer in the interest of the citizens of America.

First the facts:

In 1876, 1888, and 2000, the presidential candidate who received the most votes nationwide did not receive the most electoral votes, and therefore did not become the president.

If you're a Republican or simply a fan of George W. Bush, Gore's loss in 2000 probably made you happy, but consider how the electoral college could have screwed your guy in 2004.

If John Kerry had gotten 130,000 more votes in one state—

Ohio—he would have become the president, even though Bush would still have received three million more votes than Kerry.

Both of the last two presidential elections are perfect examples of why America's vastly changed geography and demographics have outgrown the electoral college.

Even more perplexing is the simple fact that in forty-three states, the elected delegates who cast the votes in the electoral college can legally vote any way they choose, without regard to the votes cast by the citizens who've entrusted them. And that truly makes no sense.

I mentioned earlier that I was opposed to amending the Constitution in order to restrict current freedoms, but the electoral college was not created as a guarantor of freedom. The original purpose was to guarantee that every president didn't come from the same big state—say, New York. America has since become such a large and diverse nation that the college is no longer needed.

Think about it: why should a vote cast in one hotly contested state—like Ohio or Florida—count more than a vote cast in Rhode Island or Hawaii?

Whether you're a Democrat or a Republican, deep down inside you know that the candidate who receives the most votes should be the president.

Amending our Constitution should never be done casually, and should never be done to restrict the rights and freedoms of any Americans. Ending the electoral college passes that test with flying colors, and in the long run will be good for America.

What more can you say?

The Willie Way ✏

Sages or Real People

From the ancient texts of the Tao to the teachings of the Bible and most other great books of learning, there is no one more valued than the true sage. Now I'm not claiming to be a sage, and suspect that my doing so would be an automatic forfeit of the label, but I do know that all of us need true sages to lead us through this world.

What I like most about the Tao philosopher Sun Tzu is his take on what we might refer to as sages, but what he also referred to as "real" people. Put simply, he believed in the beauty and the strength of real people. Before you start arguing that we are all real, listen to the ideas of Sun Tzu, then consider how real you have been in your life.

Real people are like still water. They are the most level thing in the world.

While most people live in a frenzy and never notice the passing of the sun or the phases of the moon, the sage IS the passing of the sun and the phases of the moon.

Real people sleep without fear, and awake without worry.

Real people comprehend what is beneficial and what is harmful.

————

Real people forget to speak.

Living in harmony with nature, real people improve their own health by their own calm.

Real people do not regret their own lot, and so do not diminish themselves through their own minds.

Though they know the value of play, they do not scheme, nor do they glorify their own success.

Real people are like others and a part of society, but are also beyond society and cannot be constrained.

We all need others, but not at the expense of who we are.

Real people know that it is impossible to hide your possessions, but all too easy to hide yourself.

Real people have more regard for reality than for rulers.

Real people honor truth and value justice for all people. Real people do not oppose minorities.

Real people praise what is good and repudiate evil.

Real people make law into a body, use courtesy as if it were wings, use knowledge as if it were a force, and trace virtue to its source.

Real people do not forget their beginnings or look for their end.

Real people know that their age is good. And that old age is also good. And that any age is good.

Alive is better than dead, as far as we know.

Whatever Happened to
Peace on Earth? ↜

This is Jimmy's tree where Jimmy liked to climb
But Jimmy went to war and something changed his mind.
　　—Willie Nelson, "Jimmy's Road"

O Lord our God, help us to tear their soldiers to bloody shreds
with our shells; help us to cover their smiling fields with the
pale forms of their patriot dead; help us to drown the thunder
of the guns with the shrieks of their wounded, writhing in
pain; help us to lay waste their humble homes with a
hurricane of fire.
　　—Mark Twain, "The War Prayer"

I've been called an outlaw for much of my career, but in all those
years I've written just two protest songs.

The first was the Vietnam era "Jimmy's Road," and though it
only contained a few short verses, it said a lot of what I felt about
the war in Vietnam and about war in general.

I believe in peace. I also believe that culture and knowledge
are capable of bringing about both freedom and peace.

That made it all the sweeter when my old friend Jimmy Carter
was awarded the Nobel Peace Prize in recognition of his *"untiring*
effort to find peaceful solutions to international conflicts, to advance

democracy and human rights, and to promote economic and social development."

So when President Carter invited me to the Nobel ceremony in Oslo, I was pleased to sing for the king of Norway and everyone else who'd gathered to honor Carter and the other new laureates.

For me, the highlight of the evening was when Carter joined me onstage and we serenaded the crowd with a duet of Jimmy's favorite song, "Georgia." I don't think there was a dry eye in the house, including ours.

More recently, the band and I traveled to Plains, Georgia, to put on an eightieth birthday concert for President Carter and all the residents of Carter's hometown. While we were there, Carter said something that really touched me.

"When I was in trouble in the White House or when I wanted to have some deep thoughts," Carter explained, "the number one thing I played was Willie Nelson songs. The good things I did as president, and the mistakes I made—you can blame half of it on Willie."

And when I look at his true record, I'm proud to accept the credit and the blame. Say what you will, Jimmy Carter is a man who believes in peace. And he hasn't spent his post-presidential years simply enjoying celebrity and playing golf. He's dedicated his time and efforts to promoting peace through conflict resolution around the world.

Knowing Carter had a little to do with my realization that "Jimmy's Road" no longer covered everything I needed to say about war and peace.

Our invasion of Iraq was part of it, too.

So shortly before Christmas 2004, I released my second protest song, "Whatever Happened to Peace on Earth"—which criticized both the war in Iraq and those who think it unpatriotic to question our government.

Reaction to the song was swift and vociferous. At my concerts, we distributed posters with the lyrics on the back, and I received an incredible amount of response from both Republicans and Democrats who agreed with our thoughts and applauded our efforts.

But this reaction was far from unanimous, and there were plenty of others who said I was un-American and that I wasn't supporting our troops. And my response to that is to point out that supporting peace doesn't mean you're against the people who risk their lives for their country. I'm just opposed to their risking their lives for what may not in the long run be any real gain.

This all started when nineteen men from Saudi Arabia attacked us. Our response was to invade Iraq. Sorry, but I still don't get it.

I've met the young men and women who are fighting this war at my concerts all across America. I've also visited our wounded troops at Brook Army Medical Center in San Antonio and Ramstein Air Force Base in Germany. I was accompanied by my *Dukes of Hazzard* costar Jessica Simpson, and if Jessica can't put a smile on the face of a young soldier, then it can't be done.

But as those soldiers called out to me and shook my hand and hugged me close, I knew more than ever that my responsibilities are to them, not to the leadership who sent them off to war.

There is a tendency in the world to think of war as inevitable. When someone says, "Those people have been fighting for a thousand years," what that person truly means is they don't have a clue why a war is being waged, why young men are dying and the resources of the earth are being destroyed.

It's so much easier to say something bad is inevitable than to do something positive as an alternative to war.

Thinking of war as inevitable turns peace into an abstract

concept, something that can't truly exist because of some basic flaw in human nature. It's an easy assumption, because thus far in human history, peace has always been temporary.

But war now holds new possibilities. For the first time in history, we have the ability—through nuclear, biological, and chemical warfare—to destroy our own race.

I'm as proud to be an American as any man alive, and believe we are the greatest nation in history. But I also believe what makes us great is not our strength of force, but the power of our ideas—and of the founding documents—which have sustained us.

The right to speak loudly and freely on any subject you choose is clearly one of the most basic principles of this great nation. Those who would silence criticism of our government's policies and actions only reveal their own shameless ignorance of what truly makes us great.

The value of open and honest debate becomes even more clear when you consider the long-term effects of each and every war this country has fought in the past fifty years. World War II was the last absolutely unavoidable war fought by this country, as well as the last war we fought where America's victory clearly resulted in a better world.

We came to a kind of victory in Korea, but the long-term result has been that North Korea remains the most isolated and potentially dangerous nation on earth. In the meantime, their chief ally at the time—China—is now our largest single trading partner and has nuclear-tipped missiles ready to fire at the U.S. What exactly did we win?

We lost 67,000 young men and women in Vietnam, and divided our nation with wounds that have still not fully healed. Isn't it time to reach across that divide and all work together for a better future?

While war may have once served the human species, it seems as if that time has past. In the days of instant communications, the World Wide Web, and vast international trade, we no longer have the excuse of fearing what we do not know.

We also no longer have the excuse of pretending that war will make us safe. Despite the end of the Cold War, there are currently 30,000 nuclear warheads on earth. Somehow we've come to the assumption that it's okay to keep that power in reserve, and simply trust that some flock of migrating geese or even the actions of a madman won't cause that power to be used.

But the truth is plain to see. Thirty thousand nuclear weapons are precisely thirty thousand too many. Many thousands of dead in Iraq—whether Americans or Iraqis—are thousands too many.

With each of those deaths, each of us has been diminished.

By the time I could walk, I already knew it by heart—"Thou shall not kill."

I once had a United States Congressman tell me why that commandment doesn't apply to us in this situation, and I had to say that I don't remember Moses writing, "Thou shall not kill . . . unless you think you have a good reason."

The Tao says that when the world lacks the Way, horses are bred for war. And when the world has the Way, horses are sent to till the fields.

Isn't it time we get back to plowing and planting the seeds of peace? I know that it's not going to be easy, but I also know that whatever effort is required will be reaped a thousand times over by our descendants.

Don't confuse caring for weakness
You can't put that label on me
The truth is my weapon of mass protection
And I believe truth sets you free.
      —Willie Nelson, "Whatever Happened to Peace
        on Earth"

Still Is Still Moving 🖎

Which of you can make yourself inert,
to become in the end, completely full of life?
      —The *Tao Te Ching*

Still is still moving to me
It's hard to explain 'cause it won't go into words.
I can be moving or I can be still
But still is still moving to me.
      —Willie Nelson, "Still Is Still Moving"

When people ask me which of the songs I've written are my favorites, "Still Is Still Moving" always comes up near the top of the list. The band and I play it at almost every concert, and I've recorded it countless times as well, so you've got to figure the song means something important to me.

Sometimes I wonder if perhaps the song is me.

Whether you look at the song from the point of view of ancient philosophies or from the modern knowledge of quantum physics, there is great motion in all stillness, and true stillness at the heart of all action.

The early Chinese philosophers referred to this in the concept of something called Wu Wei, which suggests fulfilling every task with the least necessary action. Two notes are not required when one will suffice.

Twenty words may not say something better than ten, or one. For me, that word is stillness.

No matter how still I am, the world around me is abuzz with activity, and the world within me as well. Modern physics tells us that the atoms in our body—and all the particles and forces that make up those atoms—are never at rest. While our bodies and the world around us seem solid, that physical appearance is merely an illusion, for each of our atoms is comprised primarily of empty space.

If your life in this modern world seems to pass you by at the speed of light, perhaps you should consult Einstein, who proved that the faster we travel, the more time is compressed. That's right, the faster we go, the less time we have. So what's your hurry?

This may not mean much to you, but it must be quite traumatic for the atoms. Would you like to hear an atom joke? I didn't think so, but here's one anyway.

A neutron walks into a bar and says, "How much for a beer?" And the bartender says, "For you, no charge."

While the atoms race and drink at their own pace, we also fail to notice that the slower we travel, the more time expands.

The closer you look, the more reality turns out to be an illusion.

If you touch an old book on a table, it appears to be still. But in that stillness are molecules, atoms, and particles traveling at incredible speeds.

Unless you're Carl Lewis racing for gold, the obvious solution is to slow down. Not just your body but also your mind. In the speed of your actions, you are just a blur in the mirror, but in the stillness of your mind, you may be able to find your true self.

In the stillness of your mind, you may find something larger than yourself.

God is all around us, but it takes stillness to know his message.

Sometimes in my concerts, I find that I've slipped outside of myself to the same place that I find in meditation. Like the audience, I can see myself on stage. I can see my band behind me and all around me. I can see Poodie and David Anderson in the wings, and Budrocks, Bobby Lemmons, and Josh the sound guy on the light and sound boards. All of us are connected to each other and to the audience, and whether we're all caught up in "Angel Flying Too Close to the Ground," or just rocking through "Whiskey River" for the third time of the night, that's the kind of moment that keeps me coming back on the road again and again. In that moment, I see myself, my family band, and the audience—all of us are a part of one joyful whole.

It's like the eye of a hurricane, I'm connected to everything.

Whether it's in your work, in your play, or in special times with family and friends, if you can slow down enough to step outside your body for a little look around, I suspect you'll like what you see. And if you don't, perhaps your intuitive wisdom will show you how to be the person you'd like to see.

Think of it as the opposite of Chef Emeril's "Crank it up a notch. Pow!"

Away from the hot sauce and garlic, I'd suggest you try, "Crank it down *a notch. Tao."*

To glide through life with abandon is effortless. A deep-rooted center of calm, which may be surrounded at times by a whirlwind of energy, you are the captain of your own ship, sailing toward the future.

If I were a true master and not just a guitar picker, I'd be better able to communicate the essence of this stillness. So far the best I've been able to do is to put it in a song.

> *Still is still moving to me*
> *And I swim like a fish in the sea all the time*
> *But if that's what it takes to be free I don't mind*
> *Still is still moving to me.*
> —Willie Nelson, "Still Is Still Moving"

Graduation with Honors 🖎

Nothing lasts forever,
but old Fords and a natural stone.
　　—Bobby Emmons/Chips Moman,
　　　"Old Fords and a Natural Stone"

Many years ago in Fort Worth, I used to sell Bibles door to door, though I gave it up because I felt guilty about charging more than people could afford for something that belongs to all of us. But selling Bibles had given me the opportunity to see the insides of these people's houses, and that showed me what they really needed, which was vacuum cleaners.

I felt a lot better about selling vacuums than I did Bibles. I sold a lot of Kirby vacuums and it didn't hurt my conscience because everything I said about those vacuums was the truth.

If you tell someone the truth and they fall for it, then more power to the truth.

There are a lot of salesmen in the world, and part of the key to selling something is to convince people that they need what you're peddling. Turn on the television or radio and it doesn't take long to hear somebody saying that he or she knows what God wants and what God thinks, and what God has planned for you. Nothing personal, but I'm not buying that line of vacuum cleaners this week.

*I don't think any person has any special knowledge about what
God has planned for me and you any more than you and I have.*

I grew up as a Protestant, and knew a lot about Baptists and
Methodists and Catholics, but when I was sixteen or seventeen
years old, I started realizing there might be more than I had been
taught, or thought I knew. But there were clues.

I mentioned earlier that I started writing cheating songs when
I was too young to have any idea what I was writing about. I
shouldn't have known anything about broken hearts, but there
was something inside of me that did know. To me, it seemed like
something I knew so well that perhaps I'd experienced it in another lifetime.

I also began to notice that certain things would happen to certain people who obviously didn't deserve them. And I thought
maybe that was because of something that happened to them earlier, in another lifetime.

Wondering what the rest of the world believed about these
kinds of ideas, I went to the library and began to read. And I
learned that many Eastern religions are a little easier on rating
your progress on earth. Perfection is the goal, but you get many
lifetimes to get there.

In my own church, I'd heard the preacher quote Jesus saying,
"These things I do, you'll do also. You'll be perfect as I am perfect."

But the chances of me achieving the perfection of Jesus in one
lifetime seemed pretty slim.

To me, it seems like the only way we can achieve the perfection that Jesus wanted for us is to keep at it. If we keep coming
back, we'll probably continue to make the mistakes everyone makes,
but we'll also be learning from them.

In school, you start out in the lower grades, and every year or so, you move up the ladder till you graduate. Maybe sometimes you don't pay attention and don't learn a thing—or maybe you cause more than your fair share of trouble—in which case you get held back a year, or even put back into a lower grade.

The result in school is that everyone wants oversize, overage Jimmy Joe Numbnuts to play on their football team so he'll dump a 55-gallon drum of whup-ass all over the other players who are two or three years younger than him.

The result in life is that some of us have a long ways to go to earn our way back from long-ago mistakes, and if you screw the pooch bad enough in this life—like that Charles Whitman nutcase who long ago took out a bunch of innocent college students with him on a shooting spree from the tower at the University of Texas—he may have been put back so far that he's a cockroach and won't work his way back to two legs until he's been squished quite a few times.

On the other hand, Texas also had the brilliant and compassionate Barbara Jordan, who in my book is found in the same chapters as Marie Curie, Einstein, and Gandhi, and you've got to think there's a good chance that they all graduated with honors. Maybe they don't have to come back again. Or maybe they can take one more shot at it just to show off a little.

Maybe we've already been reincarnated about a million times, and it just turns out we're slow learners.

It doesn't make sense any other way. How can we be created equal if there's a guy over here sitting on the corner, blind, with no feet, trying to make it, and there's another guy out there running around in a new Cadillac with two girls on either side of him and millions of dollars coming in?

That's when karma kicks in; you get rewards for the good, you pay for the bad. Life is like school—you get tests all the time. Some you pass, some you fail.

One of the things that makes me think I've had many former lives is that I haven't run into anything I haven't seen or heard before. I also feel as if I can put myself in the place of just about everyone I see, and that gives me the feeling that maybe I've been in their shoes before.

That's why I always advise that before you say something bad about someone, you should first walk a mile in their shoes. That way, if they get pissed off, you'll be a mile away and you'll have their shoes.

I've never tried any of those gimmicks where you try to channel who you were in a former life, because I truly don't care. This life is who I am now, and it will take all my curiosity to learn who I am now, without wasting my time on who I might have been.

The most beautiful thing about belief in reincarnation is that it gives you a very strong attitude in your approach to death. Like everyone else, I've lost friends and family who I loved beyond the description of words. And though my sorrow weighted me like a stone, I am lifted by my belief that they will be back on earth, benefiting from the good things that they did and from the love that was in their hearts. Perhaps we'll cross paths again in some future life. Our eyes might meet and a flash of recognition may pass between us.

Some of the loved ones we've lost may already be back among us, schoolchildren perhaps, in Abbott or in India. And that is all the more reason to look out for your fellow man.

Whether you believe in reincarnation or not, we are all brothers and sisters—six billion of us and counting—and the sooner we start treating one another that way, the sooner we'll graduate with honors.

I Didn't Come Here (And I Ain't Leaving) ✍

You will never find happiness
until you stop looking for it.
    —Lao Tzu, the *Tao Te Ching*

Sometimes I feel like a dinosaur in a jet fuel age. I'm seventy-two years old and every day someone asks me when I'm going to retire. But all I do is play music and golf, and I can't figure out which one they want me to give up.

Things have all been pretty good for a long time. I wouldn't want to ask for any more. On the other hand, I'll be glad to take it if it comes along.

I've had the opportunity to sing with a lot of the best singers in the world. Some of them were my heroes; many were my greatest friends. So there's nothing that I really have a burning desire to do because I've been fortunate enough to do a lot of things.

Whatever keeps me going, it's not unfulfilled ambitions. Concert tonight, another city tomorrow. Maybe record a couple of new songs next week.

It's what I do. It's who I am.

If you're thinking that I'm old enough to be offering any final words, you should forget about that right now. I'm still learning, and hope to be doing so for a good while yet. In life and in golf, it ain't over till it's over.

Besides, I don't have anything I feel I need to get off my chest. No confessions. No last-minute pleas for forgiveness.

When you've fallen as a young man from forty feet up in the trees; when you've laid down on a Nashville highway to be crushed by traffic; when your lung has collapsed in the cold waters off the shores of Hawaii—you've pretty much used up your opportunities to fear death.

But if I'd never even cut myself shaving, the way I feel about life and death would still be the same.

I don't fear death, for there is no death.

I also don't believe I've quite perfected the course, so there's no graduation yet for me.

My long-term ambitions are to make the show tomorrow night and the night after that, plus I'd like to finish this book and have the chance to hear whether people think I've given them something that might help them a bit in their lives, or whether I'm just full of shit.

In the music business and in just about every other facet of life, what you leave is who you are. And that's a thought that at some point in your life deserves a fair amount of your attention.

When I leave, I will be a lot of fine music—at least I know it was fine having the opportunity to make it. I will also be a father, grandfather, great-grandfather; a husband, a friend, and a person who cared about other people and the beautiful world I was born into.

I've had interviewers ask me how it feels to think of future generations listening to my music. And while it's nice to think that my songs—and my voice—will outlast me, the truth is, my life is just a moment in time, and my music just the record of moments in that life.

In time, though, my music will fade away to a soft, distant song, and then it will be no more. Ultimately, all of our achievements will fade away, which is why the point of our lives is not just to become famous or even to produce lasting work.

Really, when you get down to it, aren't we all just doing the best we can?

At this moment, my best is going toward getting these words right. It's a nice coincidence that this moment of mine is coinciding with a moment in your life when you read them. Here we are—connected across time and space by the thoughts we share.

And that is a thought that brings a smile to my face. How about you? I'm going to carry that smile with me until I stumble across the next one, and I hope you do the same. Connections to those around you, to the world around us all, and to the universe that stretches into the great beyond are the things that define us.

Each one of us is made of the same matter as the stars and everything else streaking out from the Big Bang that created the universe—which makes us an essential part in an endless cycle of birth and death, all of us just doing our damnedest to finally get it right.

They say the end of one road is just the beginning of another. Does that deserve a hallelujah or an amen? Perhaps both.

When in doubt, I try to remind myself that the path to God is paved with love.

Ain't It Funny
How Time Slips Away? ↙

Time flies like an arrow.
Fruit flies . . . like a banana.
   —Townes Van Zandt

So two guys drive up to the golf course, and an old man leaps nimbly forward and says, "Need a caddy?" Then he grabs their two heavy bags and sprints to the first tee.

The golfers catch up and one of them says, "Say, you're pretty spry for an elderly chap. How old are you?"

"Ninety-one!" says the caddy. "But this is nothing! This weekend I'm getting married!"

"Why would a ninety-year-old man want to get married?" one of the guys asks.

And the old man replies, "Who says I want to?"

Every few years, my pal Turk pulls out his ratty reporter's notebook and asks me one of those questions that makes me HIS canary in the coal mine.

"What's the best age?" he asks.

And so far I've always said the same thing: "This one."

So what can I say about getting older that hasn't already been said by a bunch of other old farts?

I've heard it said that you're only as old as you feel. I'd find that more of a comfort if I didn't wake up now and then feeling pretty dang old.

But most mornings, after a nice night's sleep, with Gator driving the Honeysuckle Rose a few hundred miles through the heartland of America, I can hardly wait to peek out the blinds and see where we are. One of the beauties of the bus is that we could be anywhere. I could look out the window and see endless fields of wheat, the snow of the Rocky Mountains, or the rolling waves of the Gulf Coast. If we get to the gig early enough, I may have time to sneak in nine holes of golf before the show. I'll also get to talk to a few old and new friends about what's going on in our lives and in the world. And the next thing I know, the band will be onstage and we'll be launching into "Whiskey River."

No one knows how long I'll be able to keep this pace, but I can promise I'm in no hurry to give it up.

Remember our little Einstein talk? According to the theory of relativity, you can't say "when" you are without knowing "where" you are. And as long as you keep moving, the past and the future blur until what you truly know is now.

So I try to take things not only one day at a time but one moment at a time. The only way time is on my side is if I live every moment of it fully. That doesn't mean I'm not getting old or I won't die. But knowing I made the most of what I was born with and saw and learned along the way will in the long run, I think, help me accept my own passing. Instead of fearing death, I'd like to think of it as the next step along the way.

Since we know so little of the whole, it's all the more important to know yourself. That brings us to the last question, the question that will best start your day, possibly every day, of your life.

The question is, "Who am I?"
Within the answer to that question is the thing we call happiness.

As for myself, I am just a troubadour going down the road, learning my lessons in this life so I will know better next time. I believe the lessons are out there waiting to be found, and waiting inside me to be found as well.

As the miles and miles of miles and miles roll by, I try to listen to the voice inside me as it offers advice, tells tales, and whispers the melody to what will be my next song.

Depending on the time of day and what's been bouncing around in my life, those voices may not always be in my best interest. If an inner voice says, "Tell Gator to stop the bus on the next overpass so I can determine whether I can fly or not," then I'll probably have a cup of coffee and choose to listen to some other voice.

I like it when the other voice reminds me that I am the luckiest man on earth, that I am surrounded by a very large family of people I love and who love me, and that as long as my body and this bus will carry me, I can step onstage and lift my heart in song that will carry me and my audience through the worst that life has to offer.

Knowing this may not spare me from the sorrows of life and the troubles of the world, but together—myself, my family, and my friends and fans—we use that common song in our hearts to carry on.

In the end, all of us are just angels flying close to the ground.

Returning to the words of Kahlil Gibran that I first read so many years ago, I am reminded that in our quest to return to God, each of us, in our heart, carries a map to that quest, a map that is made of love.

Love is what I live on. Love is what keeps me going.

So all I can say to you is what I've said to myself a thousand times.

"Open your heart, Willie, and give love a try. You'll be amazed at what happens."

So far, it's worked pretty well.

About the Authors ✍

WILLIE NELSON has appeared in a dozen films and on 250 albums and CDs, has written 2,500 songs, and has performed over 10,000 shows across America and around the world. He has supported numerous causes close to his heart, including America's family farmers through Farm Aid, which he cofounded twenty years ago.

Willie was awarded the Grammy Lifetime Achievement Award, is a Kennedy Center Honoree, a Texas Medal of Arts honoree, and the recipient of the B. B. King Blues Foundation Hero Award, and is a father, grandfather, and great-grandfather.

TURK PIPKIN is the author of nine books of fiction and nonfiction, including the novels *Fast Greens* and *When Angels Sing*, and the television projects "Willie Nelson—The Big Six-O" for CBS and "Willie Nelson—Still Is Still Moving" for the Emmy Award–winning PBS series *American Masters*.

As an actor, Turk has appeared in *Waiting for Guffman*, *The Sopranos*, *The Alamo*, and *Friday Night Lights*, and has also played a complete moron in two films with his friend Willie.